NATHANIEL HAWTHORNE
American Storyteller

NATHANIEL HAWTHORNE
American Storyteller

Nancy Whitelaw

620 South Elm Street, Suite 223
Greensboro, North Carolina   27406
http://www.morganreynolds.com

NATHANIEL HAWTHORNE: AMERICAN STORYTELLER

Library of Congress Cataloging-in-Publication Data

Whitelaw, Nancy.
   Nathaniel Hawthorne, American storyteller / Nancy Whitelaw.— 2nd ed.
      p. cm.
Summary: Profiles the nineteenth-century American author of such works
as "The Scarlet Letter" and "The House of Seven Gables."
Includes bibliographical references (p.) and index.
   ISBN 1-931798-04-4 (lib. bdg.)
   1. Hawthorne, Nathaniel, 1804-1864. 2. Novelists, American—19th
century—Biography. [1. Hawthorne, Nathaniel, 1804-1864. 2. Authors,
American.] I. Title.
   PS1881 .W45 2002
   813'.3—dc21

                              2002009273

Printed in the United States of America
First Edition 1996
Second Edition 2003

Oriole Park Branch
7454 W. Balmoral Ave.
Chicago, IL 60656

World Writers

Henry Wadsworth Longfellow

Nathaniel Hawthorne

Stephen Crane

F. Scott Fitzgerald

Langston Hughes

Washington Irving

Edgar Rice Burroughs

H.G. Wells

Sir Arthur Conan Doyle

Isaac Asimov

Bram Stoker

Mary Shelley

Ida Tarbell

George Orwell

Mary Wollstonecraft

Elizabeth Cary

Marguerite Henry

Dedicated with love to Marge Facklam
for all her help and encouragement.

CONTENTS

Nathaniel Hawthorne in 1840.
(Peabody Essex Museum, Salem, Massachusetts.)

Chapter One

"I Am Never Coming Home Again"

As eleven-year-old Nathaniel walked along the streets, he spoke to no one. He was busy with the two voices in his head—the storyteller and the listener.

The storyteller never ran out of ideas—a locked closet in a haunted house, a home that was overflowing with poison, a woman who lived alone in complete darkness, a minister who wore a black veil over his face. When the storyteller described a character creeping along a deserted hallway, Nathaniel crept along the street. When the storyteller told of a character rushing to escape from an evil force, Nathaniel rushed along, too.

At times, the listener interrupted. He wanted more details, or he wanted simpler language, or he simply didn't understand. The storyteller stopped where he was in the story, went back to the place that had confused the listener, and revised.

Later, back in his attic room, Nathaniel Hathorne (he later changed the spelling to Hawthorne) read anything he could get his hands on as long as it told a story. His favorite author was John Bunyan, who wrote about Christian, a pilgrim who seeks Truth. Christian faces a terrifying cast of characters, including a giant named Despair, witnesses named Envy and Superstition, and a peasant called Hypocrisy. These characters live along the path that Christian must follow, a path that winds through places with names such as the River of Death, the City of Destruction, and the Dismal Swamp.

Nathaniel spent some of his time with a private tutor. He had hurt his leg while playing ball and walked with crutches. Though doctors could find nothing wrong, Nathaniel asserted that he could not go to school. Lots of well-to-do children had private tutors in those early days of the nineteenth century, so Nathaniel easily got his way in this matter. Luckily for him, his tutor also loved books and language. In fact, his tutor was writing a dictionary while he was teaching Nathaniel.

Walking and writing in his head, reading, and working with a tutor dominated Nathaniel's life for several years. He had few friends. He had little to do with his family. Nathaniel Hawthorne was born on July 4, 1804. His ship-captain father died at sea in 1808 when Nathaniel was four years old. His mother, Elizabeth, moved into her father's home with Nathaniel and his sisters, six-year-old Elizabeth and infant Mary Louisa. Nathaniel's grandfather, Richard Manning, welcomed the little family and willingly took over their financial burdens. Still, Nathaniel's mother was unable to cope. She stayed in her room most of the day, even taking her meals alone there. Nathaniel's sister Elizabeth showed

Nathaniel's father was a ship captain who died at sea.
(Peabody Essex Museum, Salem, Massachusetts.)

little interest in him, and Mary Louisa was too young to care about him. Although the Mannings were kind and loving to the Hathornes, Nathaniel felt guilty about being dependent on them.

He wondered about his father a lot. Captain Nathaniel Hathorne had been at sea most of Nathaniel's life. Young Nathaniel probably knew more about his father from reading the captain's journals than he could remember from the infrequent visits. He particularly liked a poem his father wrote about Nathaniel's mother, whom he called Betsy:

> In Storms when clouds obscure the Sky
> And thunders roll and lightning fly
> In the Midst of all these dire alarms
> I'll think dear Betsy on thy charms.

Young Nathaniel also enjoyed his father's report of a fight in which he helped save a British ship from a French pirate. Everything about the sea appealed to Nathaniel's imagination. He lived in the seaport of Salem, Massachusetts, a town of storytellers. Ships brought in hundreds of sailors, eager to tell their stories after months of confinement in ships. They described wild storms, battles with pirates, and conflicts with natives. They told of hunger, thirst, and loneliness. They brought stories about the marketplaces where they had bought exotic goods—coffee from Arabia, cinnamon and cloves from the Spice Islands, wine from Madeira, and dates from Africa. They related stories

Hawthorne was born at Twenty-seven Union Street in Salem, Massachusetts.
(Peabody Essex Museum, Salem, Massachusetts.)

about deaths at sea. Could it be true, as many said, that the ghosts of dead sailors traveled back to Salem on their ships? Were some ships—and some sailors—under a curse? Had his father been under such a curse?

Stories of witchcraft also came to Salem on ships. In the 1700s, many West Indians had come into the port, some as slaves and some who sought work for hire. These Indians brought legends of voodoo, a belief that rituals and charms can control people in the struggle between Good and Evil. They told of witches who could cast spells, causing people to suffer physically and emotionally. These witches could evoke curses, forcing people to do evil deeds.

The residents of Salem had their own history of witchcraft dating back to their ancestors in the Massachusetts Bay Colony. Under their seventeenth century laws, anyone who was accused of communicating with the devil was a felon and would be punished by hanging. In Salem, these laws came into sharp focus in the 1690s because of two incidents. The first incident occurred when a slave of a Salem minister confessed to using witchcraft. The second incident involved a group of young girls playing games concerned with magic. After one of the girls became hysterical, a witness suggested that the girls had been bewitched. Nathaniel's story-teller mind was attracted to images such as someone signing the devil's black book, witches' circles at midnight in a forest, and the casting of spells and curses.

Sometimes Nathaniel made up stories for his sisters. He always told them in the first person as though the events had happened to him. The last line was always the same: "And I'm never coming home again."

Alone in his attic room, Nathaniel pondered these stories. Did ghosts and witches walk the streets of Salem? Did he really see a ghost passing through their front gate at dusk? Every year on November 5 he watched bonfires on Gallows Hill. These fires commemorated the witchcraft hysteria of 1692 in Salem. The Salem witchcraft trials had resulted in the hanging of nineteen women and the death by torture of another. One of Nathaniel's ancestors, John Hathorne, had been a judge at these trials. Nathaniel was told that one of the accused women placed a curse on John and all his descendants. Later he wrote about John Hathorne in "The Custom-House." He wrote that John "made himself so conspicuous in the martyrdom of the witches, that their blood may fairly be said to have left a stain upon him." Was his own family cursed? A year before Nathaniel's father died, his cousin drowned. The year after that, Nathaniel's Uncle John was declared missing at sea, and his grandfather's brother died. In 1813, Nathaniel's Grandfather Manning died of a stroke.

With his grandfather's death, Nathaniel lost the second father figure in his life. His uncle, Robert Manning, a twenty-four-year-old bachelor, became a third "father" to him. Robert was establishing a business and was often away from home. Therefore, Nathaniel was brought up in a household of women—his grandmother, two aunts, his mother and sisters, and a niece who worked as a servant.

When he was about thirteen years old, Nathaniel gave up his crutches and started school again. On his very first day back, he spoke in front of the class, a practice known as declaiming. He used flowery over-dramatic language, a technique he had studied with his tutor. The other students laughed and jeered. He refused to make speeches in class ever again. In 1818, the Mannings gave the Hathorne family a house in Maine. Suddenly, the children were free of the discipline of aunts and uncles. They roamed at will. They boated on the lake in summer and skated on it in winter.

Nathaniel grew tall and slender. He was a handsome boy with dark hair and gray eyes. Accustomed to solitude since his injury, he spent a lot of time alone in the woods and hills.

In his diary, he happily recorded his delight with the Maine woods: "Here I ran quite wild . . . fishing all day long, or shooting with an old fowling-piece; but reading a good deal, too, on the rainy days, especially in Shakspeare [sic] and *The Pilgrim's Progress*, and any poetry or light books within my reach." He noted details that caught his eye and his imagination—a smoking chimney in the rain, a field of rye in the morning mist, a sunbeam passing through a cobweb.

In the winter of 1818, he went to boarding school at Stroutwater between Boston and Portland. He stayed in a small drafty room over the parlor in the headmaster's home. His "family" became Parson Bradley, his scowling and unhappy instructor, and a few other students.

Nathaniel refused to stay there. He wrote to his mother, threatening to run away and become a sailor. Nathaniel's behavior did not surprise Uncle Robert, who believed his nephew was limited in both character and ability. He decided that Nathaniel should move back to Salem and live with the Mannings again.

Nathaniel went to a school in Salem. A few times a week, he attended dancing classes where he learned several dances. He played badminton and learned to swim. And he wrote frequent letters home, telling of his unhappiness.

He complained to his sister Mary Louisa, who now called herself simply Louisa: "I do not know what to do with myself here; I shall never be contented here I am sure." He wrote to Elizabeth: "I do find this place [Salem] most horribly dismal, and have taken to chew-

Robert Manning was Nathaniel's guardian throughout most of his childhood.
(Peabody Essex Museum, Salem, Massachusetts.)

ing tobacco with all my might, which I think raises my spirits . . . I can scarcely bear the thought of living upon Uncle Robert . . . How happy I shall feel to be able to say, 'I am Lord of myself!' " He wrote to his mother, "In five years, I shall belong to myself." Fear of his uncle's influence haunted him. At the end of almost every letter, he added a warning not to show the contents to Uncle Robert.

Despite his complaints, he found time and inspiration to read and write. He read the Waverly novels, popular fiction by Sir Walter Scott, in which characters became intrigued by status and power. He also enjoyed the classic *Arabian Nights*, supernatural myths, legends and romances. He wrote poetry to express his emotions:

> Oh earthly pomp is but a dream
> And like a meteor's short-lived gleam . . .
> And all the sons of glory soon
> Will rest beneath the mouldering stone.

In March 1820, Uncle Robert decided that Nathaniel should have a tutor to prepare him for college. For Nathaniel's tutor, Robert chose a man with a special love of literature. For his college, he chose Bowdoin, a reputable school in Maine of about one hundred students. Sixteen-year-old Nathaniel faced a big challenge. He had spent very few years in school. To be accepted in college, he had to read and write Latin, and show that he appreciated classical writers such as Virgil and Cicero.

Although Nathaniel progressed rapidly in his studies, he was unhappy. His relationship with Uncle Robert hung over him like a curse. To him, Uncle Robert was a threat, a person who controlled his life and robbed him of his very being. To make matters worse, Nathaniel disliked both his Aunt Mary and his grandmother. He fussed about everyday life. He said his grandmother served only rotting oranges. "We have to eat the bad ones first," he said, "as the good are to be kept until they are spoilt also."

One summer, he published a newspaper called the *Spectator* just for his family. On the masthead, he wrote "Edited by N. Hathorne & Co." The hand-lettered paper cost two cents and featured essays, poems, news, and advertisements. His essays were philosophical— "On Wealth," "On Benevolence," "On Industry." In his essay "On Courage," he wrote:

> I remember when I was a school boy, being somewhat disconcerted by the horrours of a battle of snow-balls, I blundered into the Enemy's ranks. No sooner did I discover my mistake than I rectified it with the greatest possible speed, and on my return to my own party, was greeted with ill-deserved praise, for daring to venture into the middle of the dread Foe.

Many of his poems focused on death: "Go to the Grave where friends are laid, / and learn how quickly mortals fade." He included a verse on the death of his cat Thomas:

Then, Oh Thomas, rest in glory!
Hallowed by thy silent grave,
Shall live, and honour o'er it wave
Long thy name in Salem's story.

He wrote an ad which he pretended was written by his Aunt Mary, who did not find it amusing:

WANTED: A HUSBAND, not above seventy years of age. None need apply unless they can produce GOOD RECOMMENDATIONS or are possessed of at least TEN thousand DOLLARS. The Applicant is YOUNG, being under FIFTY years of age, and of GREAT BEAUTY. MARY MANNING, Spinstress.

His mother tried to encourage him to study for a career, but he rejected her idea that he become a minister, saying, "I was not born to vegetate forever in one place, and to live and die as calm and tranquil as—a puddle of water." He disliked the idea of becoming a lawyer because he said there were already too many lawyers. He didn't want to be a doctor because he did not want to make money from the poor health of his acquaintances. He would like to be an author, he said. The problem was that writers did not make enough money to live on.

In October 1821, Nathaniel arrived at Bowdoin College. In less than an hour, he passed the entrance exam. A classmate later described him as "a slender lad, having a massive head, with dark, brilliant, and most expressive eyes, and a profusion of dark hair . . . his walk was square and firm, and his manner self-respecting and reserved."

His courses included reading in Greek classics, translation into Greek and Latin, and weekly Bible recitations. All students were required to attend morning and evening chapel services.

At 6:00 A.M. students were awakened for prayers. After the first recitation, they had breakfast. Following a short time for recreation, they had a two-hour study period. Then came another recitation. After dinner and exercise time, they had a second two-hour study hall. After another class, they had prayers, dinner, and relaxation. By 8:00 P.M. all students were to be studying in their rooms.

Rules were strict and prohibited loud singing and shouting, cards, billiards, gambling, taverns, and theaters. However, Nathaniel did gamble with cards, drank at Ward's Tavern, smoked, and cut classes and mandatory study halls.

Lanterloo was a popular, fast-moving card game that attracted his attention. As in poker, players could keep the hand they were dealt or take a chance on a new deal. Fifty cents was a common stake, about the price of a jug of wine or the equivalent of meals for two days. In May 1822, Nathaniel's mother received a letter from William Allen, president of Bowdoin, which began: "By the vote of the executive government of this college, it is made my duty to request your cooperation with us in the attempt to induce your son faithfully to observe the laws of this institution."

Chapter Two

"I Am Heartily Tired of Myself"

At Bowdoin, Nathaniel was caught gambling and fined fifty cents. He sent his mother a letter asking her to pay the fine. He promised her that he would not gamble again—at least not until the last week of school.

He was part of a group that created the Pot-8-O Club, students intent on filling their stomachs with potatoes and cider. The club meetings were held at Ward's Tavern. At each meeting, one member had to read either an original essay or poem. Although Nathaniel insisted that he hated public speaking, he always took his turn at speaking for his club.

He also joined the Athenian Society at Bowdoin, a club with political connections. In 1824, members supported presidential candidate Andrew Jackson, a military hero. Jackson won the election.

In his senior year, Nathaniel bought a gold watch-chain, a cane, and white gloves. "I flatter myself that I make a most splendid appearance," he wrote to his sister Elizabeth. His pleasure in his purchases did not last long. He also wrote: "All the blue devils in Hell, or wherever else they reside, have been let loose upon me. I am tired of college . . . and finally I am heartily tired of myself."

In May, he received a college bill which included a charge of two dollars for tuition and $2.36 for fines. He was fined $1.60 for cutting class, thirty-six cents for missing prayers, twenty cents for failing to hand in compositions, and twenty cents for missing church.

In September 1825, Nathaniel graduated eighteenth in a class of thirty-nine. His record showed that he was a satisfactory, although lazy, student in English. He was determined to become a writer. Hawthorne was inspired by successes of writers such as Sir Walter Scott, who wrote the popular narrative poem "Lady of the Lake" and the novels *The Lord of the Isle* and *Ivanhoe,* but he knew that fame and reputation would not come quickly.

He would have to continue to depend on the Mannings financially. And he was heading for a poorly paid dead-end career—if, indeed, writing was a career. In contrast, several of his classmates were already looking ahead to promising professions: Henry Wadsworth Longfellow would teach at his alma mater, Jonathan Cilley became an important Democratic leader in Maine, and Franklin Pierce set his sights on election to the legislature.

At this point, Nathaniel changed the spelling of his name from Hathorne to Hawthorne. Perhaps he did not want to be compared to the successful Hathorne members in his family. Perhaps he wanted to separate himself from the judgmental Hathornes who had participated in the witch trials. He moved back to Salem to live with his mother, two sisters, and some Manning aunts. He did a little clerical work for the Manning business, and he helped Robert Manning by editing articles for the *New England Farmer.* He spent the rest of his time in his familiar chamber under the eaves, writing, revising, and tearing up manuscripts. He felt comfortable in this room, he said, because this was the place where he had seen hundreds of visions which would become ideas for his stories.

He often wrote all night, enchanted with his characters and plots. After sleeping late the next morning, he visited a private library, the Salem Athenaeum. There he read on a wide variety of subjects. He read about travel, investigating the world through books such as *Adventures on the Columbia River, Ride in France,* and *Travels in Turkey.* He studied bound editions of one-hundred-year-old Boston newspapers. He was intrigued by the atmosphere of authority, guilt, and gloom in seventeenth-century Puritan New England society. He pondered over the witchcraft trials and the persecution of Quakers for their religious beliefs. He was fascinated by frequent mentions of curses.

Hawthorne took solitary walks around the town in order to observe people. Once he sat near the Salem toll bridges and watched people and carriages all day. On Sundays, he stood behind the curtain at his window and watched as the congregation headed for church.

Henry Wadsworth Longfellow was Hawthorne's classmate at Bowdoin College.
(New Hampshire Historical Society.)

Always and everywhere he made notes of what he saw and heard, and he recorded these observations in his journals and diaries. He described himself as a "Paul Pry" (an inquisitive character in a nineteenth century comedy), "hovering invisible around man and woman, witnessing their deeds, searching into their hearts." He also recorded scenes: "the picture of the town perfect in the water,—towers of churches, houses, with here and there a light gleaming near the shore above, and more faintly glimmering under water."

Three years after he graduated from Bowdoin, he published *Fanshawe,* a story of college life set in the mid-eighteenth century. It is an exaggerated story of a romantic triangle which features drunkenness, greed, rape, anger, and death. Like most writers of that time, Hawthorne published the book anonymously to safeguard against bad reviews. He probably paid one hundred dollars for publication. He received some good reviews, but shortly after the book came out Hawthorne decided that he did not like it. Like a man possessed, he destroyed all the copies he could lay his hands on and wrote to his friends, asking them to burn their copies.

He felt inspired to write a collection of tales about witchcraft and about the sea. The characters and scenes rushed at him day and night, and he hardly had time to write them down. He titled this collection *Seven Tales of My Native Land.* In a particularly passionate story, "Alice Doane's Appeal," he wrote about evil in the form of a wizard, "a small, gray, withered man, with fiendish ingenuity in devising evil, and superhuman power to execute it." When he finished the stories and

Nathaniel's college friend Jonathan Cilley later served in the U.S. House of Representatives. *(Peabody Essex Museum, Salem, Massachusetts.)*

sketches, he sent the manuscript to a publisher and immediately started on another book. A short time later, he heard from the publisher, who rejected the book. In a fit of temper, he burned the manuscript.

By the end of 1829, he had assembled another collection of stories called *Provincial Tales*. In "My Kinsman, Major Molineux," the main character discovers that the wealthy relative who is to guide his career has been tarred and feathered. In "Roger Malvin's Burial," the main character deserts a dying father-figure and lives with a sense of guilt the rest of his life. In "The Gentle Boy," a young Quaker boy witnesses the torture and death of his father. He also included "Alice Doane's Appeal." He sent his stories to Samuel Griswold Goodrich, an author and editor. He received no immediate answer, so he decided to try to sell the stories separately to literary magazines and newspapers.

His first published story, "The Hollow of the Three Hills," appeared in the *Salem Gazette* in 1830. As in his earlier stories, he explored sin and guilt and communication between the supernatural and the real world. He describes an eerie scene between an old woman and a young woman. The old woman calls up spirits that rattle chains, shriek, threaten, laugh, and cry. The story ends with a funeral procession.

He also published stories in the *Token* and *New England Magazine*. The pay varied—he received as little as $140 for fourteen contributions to *New England Magazine* and as much as thirty-five dollars for the story "The Gentle Boy" in the *Token*. Although the

stories were published anonymously as was the custom, Hawthorne admitted that he was the author when
anyone asked him.

In 1833, he traveled widely in New England with his
Uncle Samuel. During the trip, he continually wrote
down ideas for stories. In county taverns he talked to
judges, local leaders, businessmen, and farmers about
everything from the price of hay to local gossip and
politics. In Swampscott, Massachusetts, he lounged
around the general store, taking notes about the prod-
ucts—pins, sugar plums, gingerbread men, fishhooks.
He wrote about the customers, their clothing, speech,
and attitudes. He kept careful notes about scenery.

Hawthorne submitted for publication a two-volume
manuscript of short stories called *The Story-Teller*. In
these stories, the narrator has many of the same person-
ality traits as the author. He loves the sea, he is a writer,
he has no respect for fame, and he lacks self-confi-
dence. The publisher rejected the submission. Goodrich
helped him sell some of the stories separately to *Token*
and others to *New England Magazine.*

In 1835, Hawthorne published more than a dozen
stories, articles, and sketches in popular magazines.
These publications established Hawthorne's writing
reputation. His work received good reviews from the
literary men in the New England area. However, it did
not receive good reviews from Hawthorne. He said the
drama was shallow, and the humor was not funny.

In the eleven years since college graduation,
Hawthorne had prepared three collections of tales and

sketches for book publication, and all had been rejected except as single stories and sketches. All his manuscripts had appeared anonymously. Although he was becoming known as a writer in literary circles, he could not make enough money to support himself. Feeling defeated, he accepted a job in Boston as editor of the *American Magazine of Useful and Entertaining Knowledge* in 1836. The five hundred dollar a year salary appealed to him. He would no longer be dependent on the whims of editors for his pay.

Hawthorne borrowed five dollars from Uncle Robert and took the stage for Boston, where he learned to write quickly and concisely with little time or thought for creativity. His task was to fill each monthly magazine, sometimes writing as many as forty articles for one issue. He wrote brief biographies, articles, and essays. He wrote about Jerusalem, travel on an Ontario steamboat, pirates, wigs, the bells of Moscow—any subject which piqued his interest and that he could quickly research. Sometimes he added a touch of imagination, as when he created dialogue for an argument between American patriot John Adams and British King George III. After he wrote a thousand-word essay on George Washington and one on Thomas Jefferson, he decided to write a series on American presidents. In five months he wrote the equivalent of three or four books.

He did not receive any of the salary he had been promised. He asked his sister Louisa for help: "[I]f you have any money, send me a little. It is now a month since I left Salem, and not a damned cent have I had."

Because he could no longer afford to borrow books from the Boston Athenaeum, he had to do all his reading in the reading rooms. He asked his sister Elizabeth for help with the articles, telling her the work was easy, that he simply made new stories from old manuscripts in magazines. She sent manuscripts to him about topics as varied as debates in the British Parliament, machinery, and literature.

Hawthorne could not help comparing his rigorous schedule and poor financial condition with the status of his former Bowdoin classmates. One of Hawthorne's friends, Franklin Pierce, had become speaker of the U.S. House of Representatives where Jonathan Cilley was a representative. Another, Horatio Bridge, was active in Democratic politics and a wealthy contractor. Henry Longfellow was a successful poet and an instructor at Harvard. Other old school friends included a chief justice, a superintendent of schools, and a state governor. Many were married and had children. Hawthorne had no thoughts of getting married.

Four months after he began work for the *American Magazine*, he received his first salary installment—twenty dollars. In June, the company went bankrupt. Hawthorne's manuscripts were seized for the magazine's unpaid debts. He was out of a job, but Goodrich published eight of his stories in the fall edition of the *Token*. He received $108 for these manuscripts.

In August 1836, he was back at the Manning home, thirty-two years old, without money or career plans. In his journal, he wrote: "[W]hat remains? A weary and aimless life . . . and at last an obscure grave."

Chapter Three

"I Do Not Think Much of Them"

Despite his dark thoughts, Hawthorne's journals grew fat with ideas for stories:

> Some incident which should bring on a general war; and the chief actor in the incident to have something corresponding to the mischief he caused . . . to make one's own reflection in a mirror the subject of a story . . . in an old house, a mysterious knocking might be heard on the wall, where had formerly been a doorway, now bricked up . . . a person to be writing a tale, and to find that it shapes itself against his intentions; that the characters act otherwise than he thought.

He included details of scenes and characters:

> The brook flowed between the forest, a glistening and brawling water-path, illuminated by the sun . . . I saw a great fish, some six feet long, and thick in proportion, suddenly emerge its whole length, turn a

somerset, I believe, and then vanish again . . . a diminutive figure, with eyes askew, and otherwise of ungainly physiognomy . . . ill-dressed also, in a coarse blue coat, thin cotton pantaloons, and unbrushed boots.

Hawthorne started another collection of short stories and sketches. This time he chose some lighter work, hoping to attract a larger audience. He included manuscripts such as "Sights from a Steeple" in which he described himself as a Paul Pry, stories with happy endings such as "Wakefield" in which a missing husband turns up at last, and sentimental stories such as "The Gentle Boy" celebrating family love. Because he added several stories that had already been published in the *Token* and the *Knickerbocker*, he entitled this manuscript *Twice-told Tales*. Again, Hawthorne said that he was not satisfied with the stories. He could only wait to see what a publisher said.

Goodrich offered him another job in December writing a six-hundred page volume of articles on the customs of other countries for three hundred dollars. The book would be used in schools. Hawthorne refused; never again would he do such writing. He was more determined than ever to publish his fiction.

Twice-told Tales appeared on the market in March 1837. The book sold for one dollar, and Hawthorne's royalty was ten percent. By June, about two-thirds of the one thousand copies printed had been sold.

Hawthorne publicly identified himself as the author.

He wrote to former classmate Henry Longfellow that the book was "doing pretty well . . . I do not think much of them [the stories]—neither is it worth while to be ashamed of them." However, he did ask Longfellow to review the book. Longfellow did so, praising the stories as a work of genius and commending them for the way they celebrated New England history.

In the spring of 1837, Congressman Franklin Pierce tried to get Hawthorne an appointment as historian on a South Seas expedition. When this plan failed, Pierce tried get him a job as an editor or clerk in Washington. While Hawthorne waited for the appointment, he continued to keep detailed notebooks of observations and thoughts. He wrote character sketches of his friends and of people he met: "Polished, yet natural, frank, open, and straightforward, yet with a delicate feeling for the sensitiveness of his companions . . . struggling against the world, with bitter feelings in his breast, and yet talking with vivacity and gaiety."

He made notes about scenes, and was particularly fascinated with the details of old mansions: "At the angles it [an old mansion] has small circular towers; the portal is lofty and imposing."

He described in detail the outskirts of Salem, the Boston Navy Yard, and trips to Boston: "The earth looks fresh and yellow, and is penetrated by the nests of birds. Elsewhere, an old shining tree-trunk, half in and half out of the water. Perhaps an ilsand [*sic*] of gravel, long and narrow, in the center of the river."

In November 1837, Elizabeth and Louisa took him to

visit the Peabody family. The sisters pretended that this was just a neighborly visit. However, their goal was to get thirty-three-year-old Nathaniel and twenty-eight-year-old Sophia Peabody interested in each other. His sisters believed that Nathaniel was an attractive man. He was smooth-shaven with gray eyes and a square chin, a little less than five feet ten inches tall, and slim.

The match-making plan failed. Sophia stayed in her bedroom that evening. After the first unfulfilled visit, Hawthorne returned to the Peabody home and did meet Sophia. She was small and graceful with large blue eyes and chestnut brown hair. She was a semi-invalid, suffering from severe headaches, sleeplessness, fatigue, and extreme sensitivity to noise. Sometimes the clatter of silverware at a meal so disturbed her that she would eat alone in her room. She told her sister that her head ached from a variety of "corkscrews, borers, pincers, daggers, squibs, and bombs." Her mother worried about her constantly. Once, when Sophia told her mother that she had enjoyed waltzing at a party, Mrs. Peabody was alarmed. "It [waltzing] may destroy all that has been done. I trembled to read of its effects . . ."

Sophia's parents had both been teachers, and they were vitally interested in their children's education. Sophia was an exceptional student in Greek, Latin, Hebrew, French, and Italian. Drawing and painting were her special interests.

From 1833 to 1835, Sophia and her sister Mary lived on a plantation in Cuba. Sophia's family had hoped that her health might improve in the warm, island air. Enchanted with the scenery and local color, Sophia filled her diary with descriptions and her sketch pad with illustrations and portraits. She sent long and fascinating letters back to the family. Her mother had some of these descriptions printed in a book, *Cuba Journal*.

After a few meetings with both families, Hawthorne invited Sophia to take walks with him. They were always accompanied by chaperones, of course, either his sisters or hers.

Frequently, Sophia talked to Nathaniel about his writing. On one visit, she remarked that she had so enjoyed reading "The Gentle Boy," a story about a Quaker boy named Ibrahim, that she had drawn an illustration for the story. Sophia asked, "I want to know if this looks like your Ibrahim." Hawthorne replied, "He will never look otherwise to me."

In February 1838, Hawthorne's friend Jonathan Cilley was killed in a duel. In addition to feeling grief, Hawthorne morbidly wondered if Cilley's death was an omen. Cilley was the sixth of Hawthorne's Bowdoin classmates to die.

Hawthorne wrote a eulogy of Cilley for the *Democratic Review*. He had spent time that summer with his friend and had written about Cilley in his journal. Now all his notes helped him to create a poignant image, filled with personal details of the man. He wrote to Cilley's hometown postmaster, asking for the specific details and dates of Cilley's birth, jobs, and other personal information. The eulogy was very well received.

Hawthorne tried unsuccessfully to obtain an appoint-

At first, twenty-eight-year-old Sophia Peabody did not want to meet her future husband, Nathaniel Hawthorne. *(Peabody Essex Museum, Salem, Massachusetts.)*

ment as postmaster in Salem, and in July 1838, he left Boston for a three-month journey. He left no forwarding address. Sophia wrote in her diary that Hawthorne told her he planned to change his name "so that if he died, no one could be able to find his grave-stone."

Throughout his trip, Hawthorne wrote in his journal. In a section he titled "Remarkable Characters," he accumulated a gallery of characters ready to take part in his stories. His sketches included a peddler shouting his wares, an ex-lawyer becoming an alcoholic, a blacksmith, a traveling surgeon-dentist who was also a Baptist preacher, a family grieving over the death of a child. Many of his descriptions were specific: "[H]e is a dry jester, a sharp, shrewd Yankee, with a Yankee's license of honesty . . . a doctor, a stout, tall round-paunched, red-faced brutal looking old fellow, who gets drunk daily." He noted the speech of a barmaid: "Now see how nicely I'll behave. Won't you bespeak two pieces of pie?"

He also described scenes. He was particularly drawn to a lime kiln, "The marble was red-hot and burning with a bluish lambent flame, quivering up, sometimes, nearly a yard high."

One incident that remained strong in his mind was seeing a black man, respectably dressed, treated like any other man in a hotel. Perhaps this was the first time he had seen a black person who was not a slave. He also noted that he had attended at least two funerals of children (whom he did not know), and studied grave-stones in Connecticut.

Chapter Four

"Stories Grow Like Vegetables"

When Nathaniel returned to Salem, he began to visit Sophia again. He was shy, and Sophia was, like most women of the time, determined not to be aggressive. Besides, Sophia told her diary: "I never intended to have a husband. Rather I should say, I never intended any one shall have me for a wife."

In December 1838, Hawthorne dedicated "The Gentle Boy," " To Miss Sophia A. Peabody / This Little Tale / To which her Kindred Art has given Value / is respectfully inscribed / By the Author." That same month, Sophia dedicated the second volume of her *Cuba Journal*: "To Nath. Hawthorne Esqr. whose commendation and regard alone gives value to the previous journal, this closing record is inscribed by his true and affectionate friend Sophie (as the bird said) to Nathaniel." The couple talked about becoming engaged, but they needed time to gain the approval of their families. Both mothers wanted the couple to live with them.

For two years, Nathaniel and Sophia wrote to each other. Both wrote in a poetic language: "Let us content ourselves to be earthly creatures, / And hold communion of spirit in such modes as are ordained to us / By letters (dipping our pens as deep as may be into our hearts)."

For some time before they were married, they called each other husband and wife. Once, Nathaniel wrote: "Now good bye, dearest, sweetest, loveliest, holiest, truest, suitablest little wife. I worship thee." And Sophia replied: "Oh King by divine right! no one can love & reverence thee as does thy wife."

Sophia found new health and strength with her new love. She worked even harder at paintings, both originals and copies. She saved the money she earned, perhaps in preparation for married life with a man who was not financially secure.

Longfellow proposed that he and Hawthorne collaborate on a book of fairy tales. The children's book market was growing, and Longfellow believed that they might do well. Hawthorne agreed. They also talked about collaborating on a "literary paper" and later on a newspaper, but none of these ideas worked out. Longfellow decided to concentrate on poetry and translation, instead.

Hawthorne then declared that he intended to write for children, either for the mass market or for schools. He talked to members of the Board of Education in Massachusetts about writing a child's history of the United States.

Probably because his eulogy for Cilley showed that he was a loyal Democrat, Nathaniel received a political appointment in January 1839. He became measurer of coal and salt in the Boston custom-house for an annual salary of fifteen hundred dollars. He wrote to Longfellow: "I have no reason to doubt my capacity to fulfill the duties; for I don't know what they are; but, as nearly as I can understand, I shall be a sort of Port-Admiral."

Few ships entered Boston Harbor during the winter months, and Hawthorne had time to fill his journals with notes. He wrote about the people he worked with and the people who arrived in ships. He wrote about the scenes in the custom house offices. Under notes entitled "Objects on a Wharf," he summarized the scene: "[A] huge pile of cotton bales, from a New Orleans ship, twenty or thirty feet high, as high as a house. Barrels of molasses, in regular ranges; casks of linseed oil. Iron in bars landing from a vessel. Long Wharf is devoted to ponderous evil-smelling, inelegant necessaries of life."

Some days he left the offices to read at the athenaeum for hours at a time. When he had to be at the custom-house, he coped with his boredom by dreaming about his future. He planned to save as much money as he could in order to begin a writing career as soon as possible.

He completed a manuscript for children titled *Grandfather's Chair: A History for Youth,* stories supposedly told by a grandfather who sat in a favorite old oak chair. The stories begin with the Puritans leaving England for America in 1630. The owner of the chair is a Puritan who tells of the voyage. Later, a clergyman named Roger Williams gains possession of the chair and tells his story of rebellion against England. Williams was an English Puritan clergyman who asserted that the state and religion must be separate. He established the colony of Rhode Island as a community where citizens were free to worship as they wished.

Williams gives the chair to Anne Hutchinson, who tells her story of persecution to the children who gather around her. Hutchinson immigrated from England to the Massachusetts Bay Colony in 1634, where she openly expressed her belief that salvation came through God's grace independently of religious institutions and laws. She was found guilty of heresy and banished from the colony. She and her family moved to what is now part of Rhode Island. The book continues through the owners of the chair, including an adventurer, an explorer, and a conqueror. *Grandfather's Chair*, a small, three-by-five-inch book with 140 pages, was published in December 1840.

In the winter of 1839 and the spring of 1840, Elizabeth Peabody sponsored lectures in her book shop, and Hawthorne attended many of them. He became interested in an increasingly popular philosophy called *transcendentalism*, a belief that the divine is present in each person. Transcendentalists believed that individuals could transcend to an ever higher plane of understanding through the use of reason and will. Transcendentalists believed that humans were inherently wise and good. This was the opposite of the doctrine of Original Sin that Hawthorne had learned when he was young. Hawthorne could not imagine a world in which sin and guilt played an insignificant role. He believed in the innate self-interest of man, which led him to betray, deny, and deceive.

At the bookshop he met Margaret Fuller, who refused to live her life as a quiet homemaker. Fuller was a poet and a writer of articles who advocated more freedom for women. She attracted crowds of adoring fans at the book store lectures. In open defiance of socially accepted behavior, Margaret spoke and behaved with a forcefulness then acceptable only for males. One of her admirers said, "She had the intellect of a man inspired by the heart of a woman," and another that she had "the power of so magnetizing others . . . that they would lay open to her all the secrets of their nature." Margaret agreed, saying, "I find no intellect comparable to my own."

Hawthorne admitted that he admired some of her ideas, but he found her too bold, and not sufficiently feminine. A few years later, Hawthorne strongly denied the charge that his exotic character Zenobia in *The Blithedale Romance* was modeled after Fuller.

Also present at these meetings was William Ellery Channing, a poet and minister. Channing was known for his eloquent denunciations of slavery and of war. Although a Congregational Church pastor, Channing did not accept the doctrine of the inherent evil of man.

In the 1820s, he helped form the American Unitarian Association, a denomination that supported the belief in free human will and the benevolence of God. Ralph Waldo Emerson was another frequent visitor to the book shop lectures. Emerson was a poet and essayist and, like Fuller, a leading proponent of transcendentalism. He also became a minister of a Unitarian church.

Hawthorne sometimes complained that he grew tired of all the talk at these meetings. He said he preferred to sit and dream by himself. He preferred the atmosphere of his attic room he called an "owl's nest" because it was gloomy and dismal.

In January 1841, Hawthorne quit the job at the custom-house, although he had not saved enough money to carry out his retirement dreams. But he had proven that he could support himself and succeed in the world of business. Now it was time for him to work full-time on writing.

Within three months of leaving the custom-house, Nathaniel published a three-volume, condensed history of the American colonies. The trilogy included *Grandfather's Chair, Famous Old People*, and *The Liberty Tree*, all sketches of famous Americans. The books did not sell well, perhaps because his style was not appropriate for children. His *Famous Old People* begins with an invitation to young boys to enjoy playing now because soon they will study and be subject to punishment by the birch rod.

In the spring of 1841, Hawthorne changed his lifestyle completely. He joined Brook Farm, a community dedicated to working together for the good of all

Hawthorne met Margaret Fuller at Elizabeth Peabody's book shop.
(Concord Free Public Library.)

its members. They chose isolation because they feared that evil lurked in a money-oriented, industrialized society. These kinds of communities were called "utopian" because their members sought social and political perfection. Each member was required to work on the farm, in the small manufacturing shops, in the homes, or on buildings and grounds of the community.

A close social life did not seem to fit in with Hawthorne's life-long desire for privacy. Perhaps he believed it would be a unique vantage point from which to view characters for his notebook. Perhaps he wanted to postpone marriage. Perhaps he hoped that freedom from his custom-house job and the pressures of modern society would leave him time for writing. He planned to work three hours a day for the community in return for the rest of his time free for his own projects. He acknowledged that he would lose some of his independence and some of his solitude. Still, he believed that the benefits of community life would make up for this loss. Also, Brook Farm might be a perfect place to bring Sophia after they were married.

He invested one thousand dollars of his savings from his custom-house job into the community, became a trustee of the farm, and moved in. He milked cows, stacked wood for heating, and cleaned barns. He wrote humorous notes to Sophia, telling of his adventures shoveling manure and chopping hay.

He kept notes in his journal about members of the community. He described a seamstress "with a white skin, healthy as a wild flower, she is really very agreeable . . . her intellect is very ordinary and she never says

Ralph Waldo Emerson was a leader in the transcendental movement.
(Concord Free Public Library.)

anything worth hearing." In another passage, he recollected dancers in the woods "with the sunlight breaking through the overshadowing branches, and they appearing and disappearing confusedly . . . flocks of birds, schools of fish, and heaps of apples."

After five months, Nathaniel admitted that he was bored with farm chores and that he was not writing as he had expected. He confessed to an editor who was waiting for a story from him: "stories grow like vegetables, and are not manufactured like a pine table. My former stories sprung up of their own accord, out of a quiet life. Now, I have no quiet at all." Besides, he had planned to build a house for himself and Sophia there, but the community was still struggling with deeds for the farming property.

In July, Hawthorne wrote to George Hillard, a lawyer friend who had encouraged his writing, that he was unable to write in the new atmosphere. He had committed himself to work and he felt a responsibility to put in much more time than the three hours daily that he had contracted to do. He could not furnish the story he had promised earlier to send to Hillard.

In October, he left Brook Farm even though he had advanced five hundred dollars on a house to be built. He was despondent. In all, he had invested fifteen hundred dollars in Brook Farm and had no assurances that he would recoup this money. After spending months shoveling manure, carting pigs to market, milking cows, and working in pastures and fields, he had nothing to show for this labor. Once again, he had no career plans, not even a job with which he could support a wife.

Chapter Five

"I Find Myself Dreaming about Stories"

Hawthorne spent the winter and spring writing. In April 1842, he published *Biographical Stories for Children*, a book for young readers about famous people such as Benjamin Franklin and the Englishmen Dr. Samuel Johnson and Oliver Cromwell. The second edition of his *Twice-told Tales* was also published that year. This time, the selling price was $2.25 for the two-volume set, and they published fifteen hundred copies.

In May, Sophia and Nathaniel found a suitable house in Concord, Massachusetts. They planned to be married on June 27. A week before the wedding, Sophia suffered from a nervous attack, and the wedding was postponed for July 9. Sophia recovered by that date, and the two were married.

Sophia wrote to her mother that their honeymoon in Concord was "a perfect Eden . . . We are Adam and Eve," Nathaniel wrote to his sister, "We are as happy as people can be."

Because so many ministers had lived in the home they rented in Concord, Hawthorne liked to call it the Old Manse, a term for a clergy home. Old Manse was set back from the road. The garden flourished with apples, cherries, pears, currants, beans, corn, and squash. Both husband and wife were fascinated by the Concord River that ran behind their home. Nathaniel compared it to an earthworm, "The worm is sluggish, and so is the river—the river is muddy, and so is the worm—you hardly know whether either of them is alive or dead." Sophia described it as being "too lazy to keep itself clean."

They started a habit of writing in the same journal, alternating entries. They discussed their love, their lives, and their writing. Sometimes they teased and made jokes in their entries.

Hawthorne said that during that summer of 1842, a ghost visited them, occasionally rustling papers. The ghost wanted him to edit and publish some manuscripts that were stored in the attic. He was not surprised, he said, since any New England home of a certain age would surely have ghosts. He did not find any manuscripts in the attic.

In Concord he met with his writer friends Emerson, Channing, and Fuller. He met Henry David Thoreau, a naturalist, a nature writer, and a poet. Of Thoreau, he wrote in his journal, "Nature, in return for his love, seems to adopt him as her special child and shows him secrets which few others are allowed to witness." In 1846, Thoreau chose to go to jail rather than pay his poll tax, which would support the Mexican War. He wrote about his position in an essay called "Civil Disobedience" in which he advocated passive resistance as a method for protesting.

At one time when Thoreau needed money, he sold a small rowboat to Hawthorne for seven dollars. Hawthorne renamed the boat *Pond Lily* because he intended to use it to gather lilies for Sophia.

During the exceptionally cold winter, Hawthorne often skated on the river ice early in the morning before he sat down to write. He spent the rest of the morning writing until around 2 P.M. when he and Sophia had dinner together. After a trip to the post office, Hawthorne read in the Concord Athenaeum. In the evening, he often read aloud to Sophia, especially enjoying the works of poet John Milton and essayist Francis Bacon. For weeks at a time, they had no visitors.

Until the fall and winter of 1842, the Hawthornes lived fairly well off Nathaniel's investments. They raised most of their own food, cut their own wood for heating, and spent little on luxuries. However, by March 1843, money was very tight. Hawthorne worried for himself and for Sophia. Also, he believed he owed his mother and sisters a regular income, but he was unable to supply it.

Hawthorne wrote for magazines, including stories for the *Democratic Review*. He published twenty pieces in 1843 and 1844. Among the stories were "Rappaccini's Daughter," a tale of an innocent young woman who is poisoned. In "The Birthmark," also a tale of an innocent woman, Georgiana suffers because of her husband's obsession with perfection. On a much lighter note, "Monsieur Du Miroir" is a monologue of a man observing his reflection in a mirror. The narrator says about his reflection, "There is nobody in the whole circle of my acquaintance, whom I have more attentively studied, yet of whom I have less real knowledge."

He was paid little for his stories. Sales of the revised *Twice-told Tales* did not do as well as he had hoped. On the advice of an editor, Hawthorne bought up the unsold copies, planning to issue them as a new printing. "I wish Heaven would make me rich enough," he said, "to buy the copies for the purpose of burning them."

He considered, and then rejected, ideas to write a series of tales for *Boys' and Girls' Magazine,* some storybooks about myths, and a history of witchcraft. He was invited to lecture for ten dollars. Although he needed the money, he could not bring himself to speak in public. The memory of being made fun of at age thirteen was still strong.

All the while, he continued to fill his journals and notebooks with descriptions, ideas, and personalities. One theme recurred frequently, "The search of an investigator for the Unpardonable Sin—he at last finds it in his own heart and practice." He defined the unpardonable sin as intellectual pride carried to such an extreme that it let a person manipulate others for curiosity or power.

Before his old friend Horatio Bridge sailed to Africa,

Hawthorne encouraged him to write about his travels: "Allow your fancy pretty free license, and omit no heightening touches because they did not chance to happen before your eyes. If they did not happen, they at least ought, which is all that concerns you. This is the secret of all entertaining travelers." Another piece of advice was to jot down notes immediately on finding an interesting person. This person might become a character if Bridge could remember the excitement of the first impression, "Think nothing too trifling to write down."

Many of the stories he wrote in Concord were critical of society. He wrote of greed, jealousy, and a desire for power. He recorded in his journal the change in his environment as commercialism came to his part of the world. He heard the whistle of a train: "It tells a story of busy men, citizens, from the hot street . . . men of business; in short of all unquietness; and no wonder that it gives such a startling shriek, since it brings the noisy world into the midst of our slumbrous peace." Despite his concern about the loss of peace and quiet, he admitted that the new railroad might make it easier for him to commute to Boston.

In 1844, he noted in his journal that he wrote from two to four hours a day and published one or two tales or sketches a month. Some publishers took his material and then did not pay him. Three magazines went bankrupt. He wrote in his journal that he experienced "a sense of imbecility—the consciousness of a blunted pen, benumbed fingers, and a mind no longer capable of a vigorous grasp." He wondered if his writing career was cursed.

In March 1844, red-headed Una Hawthorne was born. Una was named after a character in the English poet Edmund Spenser's *The Fairie Queene*, a young girl described as bright as "the eye of heaven."

With the birth of his child, Hawthorne could no longer depend on writing as a career. He hoped to benefit from a change in administration if Democrat James Polk beat Whig John Tyler in the race for president. Polk did win, but Hawthorne did not receive the political appointment he hoped for. Sophia and Una spent much of that winter visiting with her family and friends to ease their financial situation.

Hawthorne sought help from Horatio Bridge and Senator Franklin Pierce. They suggested that Hawthorne might be able to get an appointment as consul in France, Italy, or China. Hawthorne said he would accept such a position. But politics are as unpredictable as freelance writing. The appointment never came.

A publisher asked him to supply a collection of new tales for a book. Hawthorne complained that he was not physically and emotionally able to work on the tales. Instead, he worked a little on editing a friend's travel book. The book cover read: "By an Officer of the U.S. Navy," and also the words "Edited by Nathaniel Hawthorne."

In March 1845, Nathaniel and Sophia learned that a son of the owner of Old Manse wanted to live there. They would have to move. With a glimmer of hope, Nathaniel wrote to Brook Farm, asking for repayment of the money he had invested in the house that was never built. In a court case, Hawthorne was awarded $585, but he was not able to collect the money.

They were forced to make arrangements to return to Salem to live with Nathaniel's mother and sisters until he could get a job that would provide them with their own quarters. The only optimism they felt was that maybe he would regain some of the enthusiasm he had for writing when he returned to his chamber under the eaves.

In July, their neighborhood was rocked by the disappearance of a nineteen-year-old teacher, Martha Hunt. Hawthorne helped in the search, and he was in the boat that found the woman's body. It was a gruesome scene, made even more ghastly by the discovery that her drowning was a suicide.

That same month, he, Sophia, and Una spent two weeks at the Portsmouth, New Hampshire naval yard. Several politicians were there including Franklin Pierce, and incumbent senators from Maine and New Hampshire. Hawthorne hoped to make contacts that would lead to an appointment for him. Once again, he was disappointed.

In September, they left Old Manse, still owing back rent. Hawthorne had just ten dollars in his pocket. He wrote in his journal, "We gathered up our household goods, drank a farewell cup of tea in our pleasant little breakfast-room . . . and passed forth between the tall stone gate-posts, as uncertain as the wandering Arabs where our tent might next be pitched."

When Sophia announced that she was pregnant again,

Hawthorne's financial plight grew more intense. He was determined to have a good job, their own house, and financial security before the baby's arrival.

For months he had waited for a political appointment that would give him a steady income. He knew that two positions were open in the Salem custom-house, one for surveyor and one for naval officer. He hoped that newly elected President James Polk would appoint him to one of these positions in return for his support of Democrats. But Polk did not respond to the entreaties of Hawthorne's friends who put in a good word for him. The president was busy with more pressing problems. The United States' annexation of Texas had moved the country close to war with the Mexican government, which wanted to claim Texas as their own territory. American troops were amassed on the Rio Grande River to protect United States' interests. New England abolitionists saw annexation of Texas as a pro-slavery move, and they were criticizing Polk harshly for this move. Polk needed all the support he could get from New England and he did not want to risk any political capital on new appointments in that area.

He found some hope in Horatio Bridge's determination to get him appointed surveyor at the Salem custom-house. When his name was submitted to the Democratic committees of the districts involved, Hawthorne had many recommendations including that of Franklin Pierce. But conflict about the appointment arose because other politicians supported their candidates as eagerly as Pierce did Nathaniel. Hawthorne was frustrated. He wrote to Horatio Bridge, "What a devil of a pickle I shall be in, if the baby should come, and the office should not." While he awaited the decision, he worked on his writing.

In March 1846, Hawthorne was appointed surveyor of the custom-house for four years at a salary of twelve hundred dollars a year. Immediately, Sophia ordered a black broadcloth three-piece suit for him. Hawthorne rushed to finish a collection of stories to be titled *Mosses from an Old Manse*. He sent this collection to publishers Wiley and Putnam, and asked for a one hundred dollar advance.

In his new job, Hawthorne occupied a main-floor desk in the brick Salem custom-house on Derby Wharf. Near his desk was a long tin pipe connected to other offices. He spoke through this to get the attention of the workers. From his window, he saw decaying warehouses, ships, and stores that sold sailors' wares. One part of his job involved checking cartons, barrels, and crates to see that they were properly labeled. Another duty was to supervise workers. Most of these men were hold-overs from past political appointments, and many were much older than he.

Hawthorne noted that he was little-known in the custom-house or anywhere else for that matter. However his stamp, "N. Hawthorne, Sur" took his name and title of surveyor all around the world.

He had expected to find time to write during slow hours at work. But he experienced too many interruptions. He did his best writing at home in his study on the

Nathaniel worked as the surveyor of the Salem custom-house.
(Peabody Essex Museum, Salem, Massachusetts.)

afternoons that he could get free. He told Longfellow, "Whenever I sit alone, or walk alone, I find myself dreaming about stories."

Hawthorne kept filling his journals with sketches of people he worked with and met. He wrote of one acquaintance: "With his florid cheek, his compact figure, smartly arrayed in a bright-buttoned blue coat, his brisk and vigorous step, and his hale and hearty aspect . . . His voice and laugh . . . came strutting out of his lungs like the crow of a cock."

He wrote of an older man who often told stories about food: "There were flavors on his palate that had lingered there not less than sixty years or seventy years

. . . A tenderloin of beef, a hindquarter of fowl, a sparerib of pork, a particular chicken."

Hawthorne said that he was not a strict administrator and that he hardly disturbed the dust in the sleepy offices. However, records show that he did dismiss two officers for incompetence.

In June 1846, Hawthorne announced to his sister that Julian had arrived. "A small troglodyte made his appearance here at ten minutes to six o'clock this morning, who claimed to be your nephew, and the heir of all our wealth and honors. He has dark hair and is not a great beauty at present, but is said to be a particularly fine little urchin by everybody who has seen him."

Despite the new son, his daughter and his wife, and a decent salary, Hawthorne was dissatisfied with his life. He disliked his job and the politics behind it. He was not a successful writer. He did not have publishers begging him to write. Reviews of his work were mixed; to many he was becoming known as a gloomy writer. Perhaps most important, he did not have the time he needed to create and perfect the hundreds of stories and characters waiting in his journals and in his head and heart.

Meanwhile, his friends continued to find success and status. Sophia's brother-in-law Horace Mann was elected to Congress. Franklin Pierce was commissioned a brigadier general in the army. Two former classmates were highly respected ministers. Another was a prominent lawyer; another a highly successful businessman. Longfellow was a respected college teacher and poet.

Chapter Six

"It Is Either Very Good or Very Bad"

The same month that his son was born, Hawthorne's *Mosses from an Old Manse* was published in paper wrappers. Two volumes in one edition could be bought for $1.25. The reviews were generally good, with one reviewer saying, "Hawthorne is national—national in subject, in treatment and in manner." As usual, Hawthorne was not particularly pleased with the book. He told his editor he thought it was "rather stale." He wished to write something more substantial, a long piece instead of shorter fiction. Was it another sign of a curse that Wiley and Putnam, publishers of the book, went bankrupt soon after the publication of *Mosses from an Old Manse*?

In 1847, the Hawthornes moved into a three-story house in Salem. Hawthorne was sure that a ghost haunted the front yard of their new home. Frequently, he had a vague feeling that someone or something was passing in front of the windows. He tried to catch sight of the vision with a quick sideways glance or a sudden raising of his eyes, but he was unsuccessful. Sophia suffered from this same uneasiness.

Up in his third-floor study, Hawthorne tried to write. But afternoon after afternoon passed without a single written word. In December 1848, he was able to describe his writers' block in his journal. He said that working on a story was like pulling out a tooth that was determined not to come out whole.

Finally his journals helped him. His notes on the lime kiln started him writing the story of "Ethan Brand." He pulled out his notes on life in Concord and wrote "The Old Manse." He wrote a historical sketch he called "Main Street." At last he was writing again. But he was still not satisfied with his work.

He kept up contacts with other writers. He served as corresponding secretary of the Salem Lyceum, an organization of men interested in literature. He set up lectures for their programs, including talks by Thoreau; Charles Sumner, an anti-slavery advocate; Emerson; and Daniel Webster, a candidate for president.

Zachary Taylor, a Whig, was elected president in 1848. Hawthorne expected to keep his surveyor's job at the custom-house because of his competence even though the Democrats were no longer in power. He was wrong. In June 1849, he received notice that he was dismissed. Politicians who wanted their own candidate to fill the position accused Hawthorne of "playing politics" at work. They claimed he favored Democrats although he was supposed to be non-partisan. They said he paid Democratic workers more than other workers. Hawthorne denied the charges. He declared that no one had ever complained about his work or policies. He asked friends to use their influence for him.

The conflict grew. Hawthorne quit trying to justify his work, and he left the job. As for the future, he knew only that he wanted to work with words. Maybe he could be a printer at the athenaeum.

In a short time, he and Sophia spent most of the money they had saved. Once again, Hawthorne was in dire need of cash. Sophia was calm and optimistic. She said she saw the dismissal as an opportunity for Nathaniel to return to writing. Meanwhile, she did what she could. She earned a little money decorating lamp shades, books, and screens at five and ten cents each. Customers were particularly attracted to her scenes of Rome and ancient temples.

Fortunately, a couple of editors sent Hawthorne long overdue payments for manuscripts. Then George Hillard sent a collection of money from Hawthorne's friends, a payment, he said, "of the debt we owe you for what you have done for American Literature." This support from friends and admirers allowed Nathaniel to break through the bitterness he felt over his dependence on others for financial support. Perhaps this unexpected money gave him the challenge he needed to write again.

He began to write in early September. He stayed in his room, writing both morning and afternoon. He started out with ideas for both a sketch and a short story. In the early pages of his sketch, which he titled "The Custom-

House," he wrote that he repented for his ancestors who were guilty of persecution of supposed witches. He said, "I . . . hereby take shame upon myself for their sakes and pray that any curse incurred by them . . . may be now and henceforth removed." He went on to describe his work as a surveyor, tell some of the history of the custom-house, and discuss his fellow workers.

He turned his anger over his dismissal into a manuscript that criticized the workers at the custom-house. He called them "a set of wearisome old souls, who had gathered nothing worth preservation from their varied experience of life. They seemed to have flung away all the golden grain of practical wisdom." He described the head of the custom house: "He possessed no power of thought, no depth of feeling, no troublesome sensibilities; nothing, in short, but a few commonplace instincts." He named only one official, but a reader who was familiar with the workings of the custom-house could easily identify the models for Hawthorne's characters. This would mean the end of any government job for Hawthorne. He told himself that he didn't care.

By mid-January 1850, he had completed the sketch, but continued to ponder the meaning of something he had found in the office. This discovery was a package stored away with some official papers. In the package was a piece of worn and frayed red cloth in the shape of an *A*. This mysterious piece of cloth became the centerpiece of one of his most famous books.

For his next manuscript, Hawthorne started with a 1694 Salem law. This law established the punishment for adultery—an hour on the gallows, forty lashes with a whip, and the wearing of a letter A at least two inches long. He wrote of Hester Prynne who gives birth to a baby out of wedlock, refuses to identify the father, and suffers the humiliation of wearing the A. The father of the child suffers even more than Hester. The secret guilt in his heart nearly drives him to suicide. A third character, who seems at first to be a stranger, turns out to be the incarnation of Evil. Pearl, the baby, appears to remain above it all, so far above that Hester "could not help questioning . . . whether Pearl was a human child."

Hawthorne read the manuscript, now titled "The Scarlet Letter," to Sophia. He admitted that he was overcome with emotion as he read. The final scene was particularly poignant for him. When he sent the manuscript to publishers Ticknor, Reed and Fields, he told Fields, an editor, "It is either very good or very bad—I don't know which."

Ticknor, Reed and Fields was a newly established publishing house. Fortunately for Hawthorne, it was to become one of America's most successful publishers. Unlike most American publishers, Ticknor was scrupulous about paying royalties to English authors whose books he published, as well as to Americans. This policy brought to him some of the best known English writers of the day: Alfred Lord Tennyson, a Victorian poet known for his long poem "The Princess" and shorter poems such as "The Lotus-Eaters"; Anthony Trollope, famous for his novel *The Macdermots of Ballycloran;* and William Makepeace Thackeray, known for his sa-

Hawthorne wrote *The Scarlet Letter* while living in this house on Mall Street in Salem.
(Peabody Essex Museum, Salem, Massachusetts.)

tirical novel *Vanity Fair*. James Fields brought to the company American writers Longfellow, Emerson, and Thoreau. Hawthorne hardly knew the third partner John Reed Jr., but he became good friends with Ticknor and Fields. Ticknor furthered the friendship by lending him money whenever he asked for it. They sent Hawthorne occasional gifts of wine, cigars, and special editions of books they had published. Fields promised to print twenty-five hundred copies of any work that Hawthorne sent him. Fields was one of the first American publishers to promote books with press releases to newspapers and magazines, and by sending copies to reviewers and critics. He wrote to a New York editor, "Do let us try and put that glorious genius [Hawthorne] where he properly belongs."

The day after he received the manuscript, Fields declared that he wanted to publish the story as a book. Hawthorne hesitated. He had planned to include the story in a volume of two or three long tales and a few sketches. He thought it would be less risky to include several stories in a book than to focus on just one. He suggested that Fields include the manuscript in a collection titled *Old-Time Legends.* Fields suggested again that the story be printed in a volume by itself. Hawthorne hesitated. They compromised. Under the title *The Scarlet Letter*, Fields would print "The Scarlet Letter" and the sketch "The Custom-House," although there was no relation between these two manuscripts. In March 1849, twenty-five hundred copies of *The Scarlet Letter* came off the presses.

Fields instituted a vigorous publicity campaign for the book. He suggested that excerpts be printed in the influential magazine *Literary World*, and requested numerous reviews from well-known critics and editors. Most reviews were favorable, comparing Hawthorne to the greatest writers of the world, both past and present. He was praised for his theme, his mysticism, and his beauty of language. He was also criticized. Were adultery and revenge proper subjects for a book? Was there any reason to write about such subjects instead of about a cheerful and optimistic world? Wasn't the book immoral and anti-Christian? What value was there in his introduction, "The Custom-House"?

A second printing was sold out before it was ready for delivery. In April, Ticknor, Reed & Fields published twenty-five hundred more copies of *The Scarlet Letter*. In September, they needed one thousand more.

Fields encouraged Hawthorne to write more—immediately. He wanted a new edition of *Twice-told Tales*, another volume of short stories, and perhaps another collection of children's stories.

Chapter Seven

"Thoroughly Imbued with Ink"

With his new-found money-making potential, Hawthorne determined to leave Salem. His mother had died, leaving him no reason to live there any more. He was eager to leave this town where he had felt so alone during his struggle to keep his job at the custom-house.

He found a house to rent in Lenox, Massachusetts, in the beautiful Berkshire Mountains. Sophia visited with her parents that spring while they waited for finishing touches to the house in Lenox. Hawthorne stayed in a boardinghouse in Boston. He said he needed to be without obligation to family and friends while he sorted out some of his ideas for further writing. While there, he kept a detailed journal of city life, including sketches of people who boarded and worked where he was staying. In the evenings, he often went to popular taverns and restaurants. He made copious notes about people he watched and listened to. He kept notes of ideas for stories: "A ray of sunshine, searching for an old bloodspot, through a lonely room . . . to inherit a great fortune. To inherit a great misfortune. Caresses, expressions of one sort or another, are necessary to the life of the affections, as leaves are to the life of a tree."

Nathaniel and Sophia moved the family into their home in Lenox, Massachusetts, in 1850. He began work on a new novel. He refused to tell James Fields anything about the book except that it should be ready for submission in November. Fields announced to the public that a new Hawthorne romance, then a common term for a novel about love, was on the way. The book was not ready in November. Hawthorne would say only that it might be ready in January, and that the title would be *The House of Seven Gables.*

Hawthorne had a number of reasons for not completing the book faster. He found it difficult to get into the mood of the story since the plot held a lot of flash-back. He wanted the new book to have a stronger plot and to contain more details of scenes and characters than *The Scarlet Letter.* Also on his mind was the fact that the earlier book had marked him as a writer about gloom and sin. He resolved that this new book would be more cheerful. Despite this resolution, Hawthorne wrote the saga of the Pyncheon family during the Salem witchcraft trials. A man accused of being a wizard points a finger at Colonel Pyncheon and curses, "God will give him blood to drink." Hawthorne drew from his journal idea, "To inherit a great misfortune."

He wrote regularly every morning. Sophia said that he seemed to write in the afternoons too, even when he was away from his study. Sometimes, she said, she could not trust him to watch the children because "he still is mentally engaged when out of his study."

Fields began taking orders for the book although he had not yet received the manuscript. On January 12, Hawthorne wrote to Fields that the book was "so to speak, finished; only I am hammering away a little on the roof, and doing a few odd jobs that were left incomplete." In one of his many revisions, Hawthorne changed the last three chapters. He did this to make the story more cheerful. He placed some scenes outside the gloomy house, he brought in sunny weather, and he wrote some romantic scenes.

Hawthorne stated the moral of his book in the preface, "[T]he wrong-doing of one generation lives into the successive ones." He believed that this book came more naturally to him than *The Scarlet Letter*, but might be less appealing to the public.

After he submitted *The House of Seven Gables*, Hawthorne quickly completed a series of children's stories to be included in a new version of *Twice-told Tales*.

In *A Wonder Book for Boys and Girls*, Hawthorne tells his own versions of classic stories. His narrator entertains a group of children with tales that Hawthorne told his own children, his adaptations of King Midas, (titled "The Golden Touch"), Pandora (titled "The Paradise of Children"), and Perseus and the snakes of Medusa (titled "The Gorgon's Head"). In "The Chimaera," he writes about the winged horse, Pegasus, "[S]o there

This house was the model for *The House of the Seven Gables.*
(Peabody Essex Museum, Salem, Massachusetts.)

he frisked about, in a way that it delights me to think about, fluttering his great wings as lightly as ever did a linnet [small songbird], and running little races, half on earth and half in air."

He sent this manuscript to Fields in mid-July and said, "I am going to begin to enjoy the summer now and to read foolish novels, if I can get any, and smoke cigars and think of nothing at all."

He often wrote about his children in his journals. He and six-year-old Una and four-year-old Julian spent many hours climbing trees, enjoying nature, reading aloud, and sledding and skating in the winter. Using his journal notes for "Tanglewood Fireside," Hawthorne wrote about children playing on sleds: "Down they went, full speed. But behold, half-way down, the sledge [sled] hit against a hidden stump, and flung all four passengers into a heap."

Nathaniel was particularly intrigued and puzzled by Una. He wrote in his journal, "I now and then catch an aspect of her [Una], in which I cannot believe her to be my own human child, but a spirit strangely mingled with good and evil, haunting the house where I dwell."

Hawthorne's patience was tried when Sophia took their daughter for a twenty-day trip to visit her mother, and Hawthorne was left in charge of four-year-old Julian. The day that Sophia left, Hawthorne started on a new diary, this one titled "Twenty Days with Julian & Little Bunny." At first Hawthorne found the bunny, Julian's pet, almost as irritating as Julian. He did grow a little warm toward the rabbit, but he grew increasingly annoyed with Julian's constant chatter. He told his journal that this behavior was "more than mortal father ought to be expected to endure."

A Wonder Book for Boys and Girls came out in 1851. Hawthorne was delighted when reviewers declared that the book was sunny and happy. In March 1851, a new edition of *Twice-told Tales* was published. Within a few weeks, one thousand copies had been sold. Perhaps readers did not even notice the revised preface in which Hawthorne criticized the selections, saying, "They have the pale tint of flowers that blossomed in too retired a shade."

The House of Seven Gables sold well, with over

sixty-seven hundred copies published by September. The book cost one dollar, and Hawthorne received fifteen percent royalties. Reviews were mixed, with some critics suggesting that the book was less dramatic than *The Scarlet Letter*, others praising his style, characterizations, theme, and writing skills.

That same year, Rose Hawthorne was born. Nathaniel described her as "my last and latest, my autumnal flower."

Hawthorne was not as friendly as some neighbors wished him to be. He did not always return the calls of neighbors. A few times, he sneaked out of the house when guests arrived, keeping his head down as he dashed out a back door. He did exchange visits with writers Oliver Wendell Holmes, James Russell Lowell, and Herman Melville. Melville wrote long letters to Hawthorne, discussing his writing and his philosophy of life. He was a sailor, and many of his books revolved around life at sea. He wrote a flattering review of Hawthorne's work in the important publication *Review in the Literary World*. The two became close friends. In 1851, Melville dedicated *Moby Dick* to Hawthorne, "In token of my admiration for his genius, this book is inscribed to Nathaniel Hawthorne."

Melville's *Moby Dick* did not gain literary recognition until the 1920s, seventy years after it was published. The story is a psychological masterpiece of revenge, in which Captain Ahab attempts to punish the great white whale that has torn off his leg.

After working on some short stories and sketches,

Hawthorne decided to begin another full-length book, this one to be centered in a community somewhat like Brook Farm. In preparation, he read three volumes on communal societies and then began the "brain-work" of creating characters and a plot. For the first time, he used a first-person viewpoint. The story is about secret relationships, painful confessions, and features a diabolical character who precipitates tragedy. Although he used some of his Brook Farm diary entries verbatim, Hawthorne denied that he had patterned the story on his life there. After five months of steady writing he finished this book, *The Blithedale Romance*.

When Hawthorne submitted the manuscript in May 1852, he warned the editor, "should you spy ever so many defects, I cannot promise to amend them; the metal hardens very soon after I pour it out of my melting-pot into the mould."

One reviewer said that Hawthorne was one of the most imaginative writers in the country. Another said that the book was undoubtedly the work of a genius. Some critics complained that the gruesome drowning-suicide scene was unpleasant and exaggerated. Surely it was unpleasant, but the details were not exaggerated, as Hawthorne knew from his journal notes of finding Martha Hunt's body in the river. Hawthorne said that he profited from favorable criticism of his writing, but that he paid little attention to reviewers who disagreed with him. The book sold fewer than eight thousand copies.

Hawthorne's next two books of collected short sto-

Herman Melville dedicated his masterpiece, *Moby Dick*, to Hawthorne.
(Peabody Essex Museum, Salem, Massachusetts.)

ries and sketches, *The Snow-Image* and *A Wonder-Book,* did not please him. He believed that they were not up to the high standards of his longer works. "It would, indeed, be mortifying to believe that the summertime of life has passed away, without any greater progress and improvement than is indicated here."

Hawthorne's friend Franklin Pierce was nominated the Democratic Party's candidate for president. Pierce was a shrewd politician, very much aware that his chances of election were slim. He had not distinguished himself as a brigadier general in the Mexican War or as a senator from the small state of New Hampshire. To insulate himself from some of the more difficult questions asked of contenders, he denied that he was running for president. He failed to respond to a newspaper questionnaire sent to all potential candidates about their political views. In spite of this, or perhaps because of it, he won the Democratic nomination in early June 1852.

Hawthorne offered to write a campaign biography for his friend. This was an interesting assignment for Hawthorne, who at first assumed that he was writing nonfiction. He soon discovered that a little fiction here and there would greatly enhance the truth and, he hoped, stifle some of the criticisms of his subject. For instance, at best Pierce's war record was undistinguished; at worst he was a coward who shirked his duty in the face of fire. At best he drank a lot while a student and then reformed as an adult. At worst he was an alcoholic. Late in the campaign, opponents circulated a story that at a gambling game, Pierce had been assaulted and was too cowardly to answer the attack. The story was later proven false, but not before it had damaged Pierce's reputation.

Another problem for Hawthorne was that he disagreed with Pierce's contention that radical abolitionists were responsible for the violence that threatened to tear the nation apart. He also disagreed with Pierce's support of the Fugitive Slave Law created to facilitate the capture of runaway slaves.

These were not Hawthorne's only problems. He became so frustrated with the process of gathering material from Pierce that he considered not finishing the book. His loyalty to Pierce and his determination to complete the project kept him working.

Hawthorne finished the biography, *Life of Franklin Pierce*, in late August. Pierce was pleased with it, and he encouraged the publisher to publicize it as widely as possible. Reviews were generally favorable. In November of 1852, Pierce was elected president of the United States.

Pierce won by an electoral landslide, but his victory in the popular vote was unimpressive. He was to preside over a country deeply divided by the slavery issue. Besides the difficult political situation, Pierce was beset with family problems. His eleven-year-old son was killed in a train accident shortly after Pierce's inauguration. Both parents were overcome with grief, and Pierce's wife secluded herself, attending official functions only rarely.

Hawthorne found himself besieged by office seekers

who hoped that he could convince his friend President Pierce to accommodate them. He did what he could for those he deemed worthy and discouraged the others. He spent hours with these potential candidates and wrote letters of recommendation for them. At one point, he said, "There is so much of my paper now in the President's hands that . . . I am afraid it will be going at discount."

Hawthorne didn't ask Ticknor and Fields how many copies of the book were selling or how much money he could expect from the sales. Perhaps he was afraid that the answers would discourage him. He gladly accepted the occasional check. He worked on a second *Wonder Book* which he titled *Tanglewood Tales*. Meanwhile, he was constantly on the lookout for a job with a steady salary.

He thought that he deserved another political appointment. He had written a biography that helped Pierce to gain the presidency. He had learned a lot about government work in the Salem custom-house. He was acquainted with several national politicians. He passed on the word that he might like a consulship in Liverpool.

One of the most pleasing aspects of such a job was that it would bring a regular salary, and he would receive extra fees from each ship that entered the port. He could potentially earn fifteen thousand dollars a year.

In March 1853, President Pierce appointed Hawthorne consul at Liverpool. Hawthorne planned to stay abroad for five years. During that time, he wanted to hoard as

Hawthorne had known President Franklin Pierce since their days at Bowdoin College.
(New Hampshire Historical Society.)

much of his salary as he could. When he returned to the States, he would be able to devote himself completely to writing.

In July, the Hawthorne family boarded the paddlewheel steamer *Niagara* for the Atlantic crossing. Sailors fired a salute to the new American consul to Liverpool. A cow and some hens traveled with the passengers to assure a fresh supply of milk and eggs on the eleven-day trip.

Hawthorne's Liverpool office was on the second floor of a four-story building, a poorly lit room with just a few bookshelves, a worn New Testament, and a barometer that always registered "Fair." As he noted in his journal, he found the work boring. He oversaw quarantine regulations, checked on licenses issued by the marine board, and recorded the number and tonnage of North American vessels built and registered at Liverpool. He also met traveling Americans, talked to ships' captains, attended grand dinners, and represented America at funerals.

In some cases, he was asked to judge whether a person should receive funds or a job. "It is only one-eyed people who live to advise," he said. "When a man opens both his eyes, he generally sees about as many reasons for acting in any one way as in any other, and quite as many for acting in neither."

Another part of his job was to give speeches. Hawthorne had conquered the fear of speaking he had held since elementary school. Now he bragged that he could speak anywhere as long as he had enough cham-

Hawthorne (center) with his publishers James Fields (left) and W.D. Ticknor (right).
(Peabody Essex Museum, Salem, Massachusetts.)

pagne or port during dinner to help him through the speech. He was not proud of his public speaking, he said, although most people praised his performances. He wrote a sketch about public speaking called "Civic Banquets," which was published in the *Atlantic Monthly*. In this sketch, he told of speaking at a dinner for the Lord Mayor of London. Hawthorne complimented the Lord Mayor, and, as he wrote, "I got upon my legs to save both countries, or perish in the attempt. The tables roared and thundered at me, and suddenly were silent again."

One of the saddest of his duties was to report cases of mistreated American-born sailors who suffered torture, beatings, and sometimes murder while in Great Britain. He sent reports to the State Department year after year in vain requests for help.

In his social life, Hawthorne met prominent English writers such as Alfred Tennyson, poet laureate of England; Leigh Hunt, lyrical poet; and the Romantic poets Elizabeth Barrett Browning and her husband, Robert Browning. These authors knew and admired Hawthorne's work. Other less-well-known authors sometimes invited Hawthorne to their homes. He always refused, saying that he was "an absurdly shy sort of person."

Hawthorne had little time and no inclination to write sketches or to begin another romance. But he did fill his journal with three hundred thousand words. As always, his mind was open to literary possibilities. He was scornful of many English women: "The grim red-faced

Monsters! Surely a man would be justified in murdering them—in taking a sharp knife and cutting away their mountainous flesh, until he had brought them into reasonable shape." He wrote vividly of the shops: "The toy-shops and the confectioners, the latter ornamenting their windows with a profusion of bonbons and all manner of pigmy figures in sugar; the former exhibiting Christmas trees hung with rich and gaudy fruit." He described the meat markets at Christmas: "fat sheep, with their wooly heads and tails still on, and stars and other devices ingeniously wrought on the quarters; fat pigs adorned with flowers." He wrote of a man who continually sought his help, "Homeless on this foreign shore, looking always toward his country, coming again and again to the point whence so many set sail." He considered England as "our old home," and he was ever aware of the English heritage in America.

He quickly tired of the diplomat's life. He complained to Ticknor and Fields that he was sick of the whole job and longed to write again, "When once a man is thoroughly imbued with ink, he never can wash out the stain."

Chapter Eight

"The Devil Himself Always Seems to Get in My Inkstand"

In December 1853, Hawthorne used his own money to pay for clothing and provisions for American troops that had been shipwrecked in the Atlantic. Later, he was stunned to discover that American newspapers reported he had refused to help the victims. One reporter even suggested that Hawthorne should have a scarlet letter branded on his forehead. Although angry, Nathaniel decided that he would get more bad publicity from refuting the charge than from ignoring it.

In 1854, Congress discussed revising the pay of consuls so that each one received only a fixed salary. Under this law, Hawthorne would no longer receive extra fees for each ship using the port. Congress did not understand the high cost of living abroad, he said. Furthermore, they did not know how many Americans he helped out of his own pocket because consular funds were not available. Few of these "loans" were repaid. Hawthorne said that if the government chose to starve the consul, that meant many Americans who relied on the consul's help would also starve.

The new salary plan was passed in early 1855. Hawthorne hoped that Pierce would not institute the change immediately. He wanted to spend as much time as he could in England. He enjoyed the money and the literary friends he had met. Also, he did not want to get back to American literary circles because, he said, "America is now wholly given over to a d----d mob of scribbling women, and I should have no chance of success while the public taste is occupied with their trash—and should be ashamed of myself if I did succeed."

Herman Melville visited in the fall of 1856. Hawthorne enjoyed his company and recorded in his journal a sketch of Melville that is typical Hawthorne—questioning and probing: "He can neither believe nor be comfortable in his unbelief; and he is too honest and courageous not to try to do one or the other."

Sophia suffered from the cold and wet British winters. When her father died, the grief seemed to increase her ill health. She developed a persistent cough that worried Hawthorne. Hoping the warmer weather would help, Hawthorne sent her to Portugal for the winter.

While Sophia was gone, Hawthorne spent more time with his journals. He wrote of his loneliness: "I sleep ill, lying awake late at night to think sad thoughts, and to imagine somber things . . . Life seems so purposeless as not to be worth the trouble of carrying it on any further." He wrote to Sophia: "Thou *never* again shalt go away anywhere without me. My two arms will be thy tropics and my breast thy equator; and from henceforth forever, I will keep thee a great deal too warm."

He was disturbed with the political situation in America, where the slavery issue dominated. President Pierce endorsed the Kansas-Nebraska Act of 1854 which left all questions about slavery up to the voters in the new territory. Instead of cooling the arguments, the act inflamed riots and massacres led by protestors on both sides. Pro-slavery terrorists conducted murderous raids to capture or recapture slaves. For two years, "Bleeding Kansas" was the focus of heated debates about slavery. Around the second anniversary of the Kansas-Nebraska Act, Senator Charles Sumner gave an impassioned speech titled "The Crime against Kansas." He called upon the Senate to make restitution for the crime of embracing slavery. He accused slaveholding interests of fraud in their quest for slaves. He criticized many of his political foes. One day Congressman Preston Brooks of South Carolina entered Sumner's office and beat him over the head and shoulders with a cane until Sumner lost consciousness. Hawthorne wrote to a friend: "If it were not for my children, I should probably never re-turn . . . In my opinion, we [Americans] are the most miserable people on earth."

He was even more agitated to receive letters from Elizabeth, Sophia's sister. Elizabeth was a strong abo-litionist, and she wanted Sophia, Nathaniel, and every-one else to agree with her views. Hawthorne wrote to her, "[L]ike every other abolitionist, you look at matters with an awful squint, which distorts everything within your line of vision." Hawthorne said that he did not care for abolitionists, but if he had to choose, he would go with the North. He felt that it was time for Northerners to take a stand.

Pierce did not achieve the expected peaceful settlement of the conflict between Northerners and Southerners and failed to earn the Democratic nomination in 1856. The Democrats chose instead James Buchanan, who won the election.

Hawthorne sent his letter of resignation in February 1857, requesting that he be allowed to leave his office in August. Before he left, he made one more attempt to protect American sailors, but he was not successful. Despite his problems with the State Department on this issue, Hawthorne left the consulate with an excellent record. He had helped scores of individuals, spoken out for justice and humanity, and created long-range programs for the improvement of maritime service.

The Hawthornes left England in January 1858, bound for Italy. A visit to Rome had long been Sophia's dream, and Hawthorne was delighted to fulfill it with her. On the way, they spent some time in Paris, where they met Maria Mitchell, an American astronomer. They agreed to travel to Rome with her.

February was the season of the Roman carnival, when crowds gathered in the streets wearing costumes and masks, throwing flowers, singing, and dancing. Sophia spent part of each day sketching. She and Maria Mitchell enjoyed touring the city. Feeling guilty for his lack of interest, Hawthorne wrote in his journal, "Either the masques were not very funny, or I was in no funny mood." He admitted that he hated sight-seeing. He watched his children fully enjoying the sights: "Only the young ought to write descriptions of such scenes. My cold criticism chills the life out of it." He much preferred to walk the streets alone, watching people, and gathering information for his notebooks.

He did find some interest in art. He went from one artist's studio to another, meeting the artists and studying their work. He believed that writers and artists have something in common—they both focus on a dramatic subject, they add detail to this subject, and they both capture a mood.

Confession booths in the cathedrals fascinated Hawthorne, too. "If I had had a murder on my conscience or any other great sin, I think I should have been inclined to kneel down there, and pour it into the safe secrecy of the confessional."

He visited the catacombs, subterranean burial vaults decorated with centuries-old paintings. He noted that there was very little a person could do with a dead body. He said he wished a body might disappear like "vanishing bubbles."

He was struck by the beauty of a faun in a sculpture garden and described his experience in his notebook: "The idea keeps returning to me of writing a little Romance about it . . . so I will describe it here . . . the faun is the image of a young man, leaning with one arm upon the trunk or stump of the tree . . . a voluptuous mouth, that seems almost (not quite) to smile outright; in short the whole person conveys the idea of an amiable and sensual nature." He saw the faun as the ultimate in beauty and innocence, like man before the Fall.

During the trip, sixteen-year-old Una Hawthorne became ill with a high fever and occasional delirium. The doctors said that this was Roman fever, a common sickness (now called malaria.) Una remained dangerously ill for months. Hawthorne began to doubt if she would ever recover. In a book he was working on at the time, Hawthorne wrote about Rome, "[I]f you come hither in summer, and stray through these glades in the golden sunset, fever walks arm in arm with you, and death awaits you at the end of the dim vista." Finally, Una's fever broke. After several months' recovery, she seemed once again on the road to good health.

By July, Hawthorne yearned for time by himself to outline plots, conceive characters, and get back to serious writing. He told his journal that he needed monotony in his life so that he could live in the world within him. "Rest, rest, rest! There is nothing else so desirable; and I sometimes fancy, but only half in earnest, how pleasant it would be to be six feet under ground, and let the grass grow over me."

He did find time to be alone, but he did not rest. He worked on his story about the marble faun. The protagonist, Donatello, has some of the appearance and much of the innocence of a faun. After he falls under the spell of Miriam, he is consumed by guilt and love and haunted by his struggle between good and evil.

The Hawthornes were ready to return to their native land. But Fields advised them to live in England again first. Fields wanted an English copyright on the book about the faun. To obtain this copyright, Hawthorne had to be a resident in England on the date that the book was published. Hawthorne predicted that the book would be ready in about a year. He admitted to Fields that the book was not a cheerful one, "but the Devil himself always seems to get into my inkstand, and I can only exorcise him by pensful at a time."

Hawthorne had mentioned Sophia's travel writing to Fields, and the editor asked her to contribute to the *Atlantic Monthly*. Sophia declined, probably because she agreed with Hawthorne's opinion that writing for publication was unbecoming for a woman. He also said he believed that most women's writing was weaker than most men's writing.

In June 1859, the family returned to England. Hawthorne settled into a routine of writing five to six hours a day, producing thirty to forty pages a week. His romance about the faun was, like so many of his stories, a tale of crime, guilt, and emotional torment. By September 10, he asked Sophia to read what he had written. Sophia was delighted with the manuscript. Hawthorne said he wavered between liking it and considering it pure nonsense.

On November 8, Nathaniel finished the book, which was over five hundred pages long. He suggested several different titles, none of which really appealed to

Hawthorne's three children (from left to right): Una, Julian, and Rose.
(Peabody Essex Museum, Salem, Massachusetts.)

him. Fields sent it to the English publishers Smith, Elder & Company.

When Smith, Elder named the book *Transformation*, Hawthorne declared it a stupid title. The publishers said that Hawthorne himself had suggested that title at one point. *Transformation* was published in England in 1860. The book was published in America under the title *The Marble Faun: A Romance of Monte Beni.*

Reviews of *The Marble Faun* were generally excellent. Some reviewers said that Hawthorne was one of the finest authors of all time. But some critics said they didn't like the open-ended resolution. By the end of the year, 14,500 volumes had been printed, more than the combination of all his previous sales.

Hawthorne was ambivalent about returning to America. On one hand, he was disgusted with news of American politics. With presidential elections coming up in the fall, the slavery issue had polarized the country. On the other hand, he wanted his children to grow up in their native land. Una was sixteen, Julian fourteen, and Rose nine. As for himself, he declared that his seven years abroad had made no difference in him except that he now wore an Italian-style moustache.

Chapter Nine

"I Have Not the Least Notion"

Back in America in 1860, Hawthorne immediately arranged to move into Wayside, a house in Concord, Massachusetts. He had a new wing built to include a tower room for a study. He also added a guest room and a library. His alterations proved to be so expensive that he asked Ticknor and Fields for an advance of $550. Even with that money, he said he could not afford to buy books for the library. To hide this omission, he put up silk curtains in some spots and painted rows of faux books in others.

Hawthorne enrolled fourteen-year-old Julian in a private school in preparation for Harvard. Sophia allowed this, but she complained that Julian should not attend a coeducational school, especially one which offered dances, picnics, and other social entertainment. Neither Hawthorne nor Sophia wanted their daughters to attend such a school.

Hawthorne attended meetings of the Saturday Club,

an organization of writers that met monthly for dinner and conversation. At these meetings, he renewed acquaintance with Longfellow, Emerson, and others he had known before his stay abroad. But usually he ate his food quickly, kept his eyes on his plate, and spoke to no one. Except for this scheduled meeting, Hawthorne spent most of his time by himself. He still often disappeared when visitors called.

Fields told of relaxing with Hawthorne by the Concord River one afternoon, when Hawthorne heard footsteps. "Heaven help me. Mr. —— is close upon us," he shouted. He ducked down and told Fields to do the same.

Although he didn't speak much, he looked and listened—and told all to his journal. An example is a thumbnail sketch he wrote of Thoreau: "[H]e is not an agreeable person; and in his presence one feels ashamed of having any money, or a hour to live in, or so much as two coats to wear, or of having written a book that the public will read."

He did publish two articles, based on his journal notes, in the *Atlantic Monthly.* At Fields's urging, Hawthorne published several sketches in the magazine. His pay increased from one hundred dollars to two hundred dollars each.

When the Civil War began in 1861, Hawthorne regretted that he could not fight for his country, but he felt relief that Julian was too young to do so. He believed that the Union had never been truly united, and that it was time for both North and South to admit it.

Since his return to America, Hawthorne had not been able to write anything that pleased him. He tried writing several different novels but gave up on each of them.

When he did try to write, he insisted on high standards for himself. He wanted every sentence to be understood and felt. Sometimes he wrote notes on the margins of his manuscripts, criticizing himself for dull, awkward, uninspired writing. His comments were unsparing: "What unimaginable nonsense! . . . All this amounts to just nothing . . . I have not the least notion how to get on."

In March 1862, Hawthorne went to Washington with Ticknor, hoping that the change in scene would inspire him to break out of the doldrums. He waited with a Massachusetts delegation to present an ivory-handled whip to President Lincoln. Lincoln appeared briefly, accepted the whip as an emblem of peace, and left. Hawthorne was disappointed with the president's dress and appearance. Also, he had hoped in vain that Lincoln would tell at least one of the tales for which he was well-known.

He visited some confederate prisoners, walked over the remains of a bloody battle ground at Manassas, saw starving and bewildered fugitive slaves, and despaired about the killing of men and devastation of land and buildings.

In July 1862, Hawthorne sent Fields a report on his trip titled "Chiefly About War Matters" with the byline, "A Peaceable Man." Fields objected to some parts of the manuscript. He asked him to delete his criticism of the president's awkwardness and his sloppy dress. He objected also to Hawthorne's kindly remarks about the confederates. Hawthorne responded: "Though I think you are wrong, I am going to comply with your request."

In the winter of 1862 and 1863, he visited no one, and received few visitors. He told Fields he might visit him in Boston, but added, "I have now been a hermit so long that the thought affects me somewhat as it would to invite a lobster or crab to step out of his shell."

Fields asked for more of Hawthorne's English journals since "Chiefly About War Matters" was so well-received. So Hawthorne sent him "Leamington Spa" which was published in October. This was so popular that Hawthorne sent "About Warwick" for the December issue. Fields then offered one hundred dollars for articles ten pages or shorter and an additional ten dollars for those which were longer than ten pages. He also asked Hawthorne to consider gathering his English journals into a book.

In 1863, Hawthorne published a collection of stories and sketches drawn from notes taken while he was a consul. He published these in America and in England under the title *Our Old Home*. He dedicated the book to former President Franklin Pierce, who had arranged the consular appointment for him.

Fields objected to the dedication. At that time, Pierce was speaking out against Lincoln's suppression of free speech and the right of trial. Fields said that Pierce was so unpopular that the dedication would hurt sales.

Hawthorne in 1860, after his return from Great Britain.
(Peabody Essex Museum, Salem, Massachusetts.)

Hawthorne told Fields that he could not, in good conscience, withdraw the dedication.

Our Old Home was well-received in America, and by September there were fifty-five hundred copies in print. The dedication, as well as Hawthorne's criticism of the consulate, helped its popularity. The reaction was different in England. Some descriptions particularly enraged the British, such as his comment that the older women were: "[S]o massive, not seemingly with pure fat, but with solid beef, making an awful ponderosity of frame. You think of them as composed of sirloins, and with broad and thick steaks on their immense rears."

Hawthorne wrote to an English friend that he was weary of the war. He had not supported it in the beginning and was sure that only a victory devastating to both sides would bring it to an end. He did collect some public relations cards of Lincoln to send to his friends, saying that he believed that "Abe" was an honest man. Except for this, there was little about Lincoln that interested him.

Late in 1863, Hawthorne feared that he would not have enough money to live on, so he began working on a romance that he had begun three years before. He had many journal sketches to use, including some he had written in Italy and England. These journals furnished the material for two of his characters—an American seeking his roots and a sculptor. His theme was the search for everlasting life. In the fall of 1863, he sent Fields the first chapter of *The Dolliver Romance*. It was published in the *Atlantic Monthly* as the first of many serialized episodes.

Wayside was Hawthorne's home during the last years of his life.
(Concord Free Public Library.)

Hawthorne's health began to fail. He had alternating periods of restlessness and utter fatigue. Most of the time, he could neither read nor write. He refused to see a doctor.

In February, Hawthorne sent a note to Fields, admitting that he could write no more. He gave Fields some glib suggestions for announcing his retirement in the *Atlantic Monthly,* such as, "Mr. Hawthorne's brain is addled at last, and much to our satisfaction, he tells us that he cannot possibly go on with the Romance announced on the cover of the Jan. magazine." He added, "Say anything you like, in short, though I really don't believe that the Public will care what you say."

In March, Hawthorne traveled south with Ticknor,

hoping that his health would improve with a warmer climate. However, he hardly had enough energy to make the trip. People he visited in Boston remarked on his burning eyes and his poor hearing.

When Ticknor died on their trip, Hawthorne was convinced that death had taken the wrong man. He slipped in and out of rationality. He broke down completely when he arrived back in Concord. Sophia described her husband, "[H]e has wasted away very much, and the suns in his eyes are collapsed, and he has had no spirits, no appetite, and very little sleep." By May, when Pierce visited, Hawthorne could walk only with difficulty. He said he suffered from pain, indigestion, and general unease. One doctor suggested that he had a stomach ulcer which had become malignant. He told one friend that his biggest worry was that he would lose his mind. He feared that his inability to write would become an inability to think.

On May 12, 1864, while he and Pierce were traveling to Concord, fifty-nine-year-old Hawthorne died in his sleep.

In 1825, Nathaniel Hawthorne seemed to have little chance of becoming a writer. His family background gave him no inspiration; his ancestors had been adventurers, sailors, businessmen, and political appointees. His college work did not prepare him; his English professors judged him a lazy student. His family and friends scoffed at the idea of a writing career. Citizens of his home town of Salem, Massachusetts, showed no interest in a literary man; they focused on the excitement of living in a major seaport.

Hawthorne taught himself to write. He read everything he could find—books, newspapers, histories, encyclopedias, magazines. He spent hours watching people and listening to them—in the city market, along the beaches, at the stage coach stops, in taverns. He recorded his observations of actions, scenes, and dialogue in his notebooks and journals.

He was his own harshest critic. Even when others praised his work, Hawthorne found much fault with it.

He published stories and sketches in newspapers and in popular literary magazines. He could not earn enough to make a living. He worked for hire, writing articles for encyclopedic publications. He still could not make a living.

He accepted a number of different jobs in government service so that he could support his wife and family. He kept writing in his journals, and he kept fast to his dream of becoming a writer.

Hawthorne was self-taught and self-inspired. He wrote four novels and over seventy stories and sketches. He became one of the greatest writers in America.

Timeline

1804—Born in Salem, Massachusetts, on July 4
1821—Begins studies at Bowdoin College, Maine
1828—Publishes *Fanshawe,* his first novel
1828—Publishes about fifty stories and sketches until 1836
1837—Publishes *Twice-told Tales*
1839—Accepts appointment as weigher at Boston custom-house
1842—Marries Sophia A. Peabody
1846—Accepts appointment as surveyor at Salem custom-house
1849—Dismissed from Salem custom-house; publishes *The Scarlet Letter*
1851—Publishes *The House of Seven Gables*
1852—Publishes *The Blithedale Romance*
1853—Appointed American consul at Liverpool
1860—Publishes *The Marble Faun*
1864—Dies in Plymouth, New Hampshire on May 12

Sources

CHAPTER ONE: "I Am Never Coming Home Again"

p. 12, "In Storms when clouds obscure the Sky . . ." Ibid., 24.

p. 14, "And I'm never coming home again." Edwin H. Miller, *Salem Is My Dwelling Place: A Life of Nathaniel Hawthorne* (Iowa City: University of Iowa Press, 1991), 26.

p. 14, "made himself so conspicuous . . ." Nathaniel Hawthorne, *The Scarlet Letter* (New York: Penguin Books, 1983), 12.

p. 16, "Here I ran quite wild . . ." Arlin Turner, *Nathaniel Hawthorne: A Biography* (New York: Oxford University Press, 1980), 21.

p. 16, "I do not know what to do . . ." Miller, *Dwelling Place*, 52.

p. 16, "I do find this place . . ." Ibid., 54.

p. 18, "In five years . . ." James Mellow, *Nathaniel Hawthorne in His Times* (Boston: Houghton Mifflin Co., 1980), 16.

p. 18, "Oh earthly pomp is but a dream . . ." Robert Cantwell, *Nathaniel Hawthorne: The American Years* (New York: Rinehart & Co., Inc., 1948), 49.

p. 19, "We have to eat the bad ones . . ." Mellow, *His Times*, 17.

p. 19, "I remember when I was . . ." Nathaniel Hawthorne, *Spectator*.

p. 19, "Go to the Grave . . ." Miller, *Dwelling Place*, 57.

p. 20, "Then, Oh Thomas, rest in glory! . . ." Hawthorne, *Spectator*.

p. 20, "WANTED: A HUSBAND . . ." Ibid.

p. 20, "I was not born to vegetate . . ." Mellow, *His Times*, 25.

p. 20, "a slender lad, having a massive head . . ." Horatio Bridge, *Personal Recollections of Nathaniel Hawthorne* (New York: Haskell House Publishers, Ltd., 1968), 4.

p. 21, "By the vote of the executive government . . ." William Allen, letter to Elizabeth Hathorne, May 29, 1822.

CHAPTER TWO: "I Am Heartily Tired of Myself"

p. 22, "I flatter myself . . . All the blue devils . . ." Miller, *Dwelling Place,* 73.

p. 26, "hovering invisible around man . . ." Nathaniel Hawthorne. *The American Notebooks* (New Haven: Yale University Press, 1932), lxi.

p. 26, "the picture of the town . . ." Miller, *Dwelling Place*, 87.

p. 26, "a small, gray, withered man . . ." Nathaniel Hawthorne, *The Complete Short Stories of Nathaniel Hawthorne* (New York: Hanover House, 1959), 559.

p. 30, "[I]f you have any money . . ." Nathaniel Hawthorne, letter to Louisa Hawthorne, February 2, 1856

p. 31, "[W]hat remains? . . ." Turner, *A Biography*, 82.

CHAPTER THREE: "I Do Not Think Much of Them"

p. 32, "Some incident which should bring . . ." Nathaniel Hawthorne, *The Portable Hawthorne*, ed. Malcolm Cowley (New York: Viking Penguin, 1948), 611-614.

p. 32, "The brook flowed . . ." Hawthorne, *American Notebooks*, 6-11.

p. 34, "doing pretty well . . ." Mellow, *His Times*, 79.

p. 34, "Polished, yet natural . . ." Hawthorne, *American Notebooks,* 2.

p. 34, "At the angles . . ." Ibid., 8.

p. 34, "The earth looks fresh and yellow . . ." Ibid., 13.

p. 35, "corkscrews, borers, pincers . . ." Mellow, *His Times*, 141.

p. 35, "It [waltzing] may destroy . . ." Ibid., 136.

p. 36, "I want to know . . . He will never . . ." Louise H. Tharp, *The Peabody Sisters of Salem* (Boston: Little, Brown and Co., 1950), 119.

p. 38, "so that if he died . . ." Miller, *Dwelling Place*, 157.

p. 38, "[H]e is a dry jester . . . Now see how nicely . . ." Hawthorne, *American Notebooks,* 45.

p. 38, "The marble was red-hot . . ." Cantwell, *American Years*, 283.

CHAPTER FOUR: "Stories Grow Like Vegetables"

p. 39, "I never intended . . ." Miller, *Dwelling Place*, 143.

p. 39, "To Miss Sophia A. Peabody . . ." Tharp, *Peabody Sisters*, 119.

p. 39, "To Nath. Hawthorne, Esqr . . ." Ibid., 120.

p. 40, "Let us content ourselves . . ." Cantwell, *American Years*, 297.

p. 40, "Now good bye, dearest . . ." Miller, *Dwelling Place*, 183.

p. 41, "I have no reason to doubt . . ." Ibid., 169.

p. 41, "[A] huge pile . . ." Mellow, *His Times*, 162.

p. 43, "She had the intellect . . . comparable to my own." Miller, *Dwelling Place*, 231.

p. 47, "with a white skin . . ." Mellow, *His Times*, 191.

p. 48, "stories grow like vegetables . . ." Ibid., 187.

CHAPTER FIVE: "I Find Myself Dreaming about Stories"

p. 49, "a perfect Eden . . ." Miller, *Dwelling Place*, 207.

p. 49, "We are as happy . . ." Ibid., 207.

p. 50, "The worm is sluggish . . ." Ibid., 209.

p. 50, "Nature, in return for his love . . ." Cantwell, *American Years*, 361.

p. 52, "There is nobody in the whole circle . . ." Hawthorne, *Complete Short Stories,* 281.

p. 52, "I wish Heaven would . . ." Miller, *Dwelling Place*, 238.

p. 52, "The search of an investigator . . ." Mellow, *His Times*, 284.

p. 53, "Allow your fancy . . ." Cantwell, *American Years*, 379.

p. 53, "Think nothing too trifling . . ." Ibid., 379.

p. 53, "It tells a story . . ." Mellow, *His Times*, 244.

p. 53, "a sense of imbecility . . ." Ibid., 232.

p. 55, "We gathered up our household goods . . ." Ibid., 265.

p. 57, "What a devil of a pickle . . ." Turner, *A Biography*, 171.

p. 58, "Whenever I sit alone . . ." Ibid., 175-6.

p. 58, "With his florid cheek . . ." Cantwell, *American Years*, 404.

p. 58, "There were flavors on his palate . . ." Ibid., 405.

p. 59, "A small troglodyte . . ." Miller, *Dwelling Place*, 259.

CHAPTER SIX: "It Is Either Very Good or Very Bad"

p. 60, "Hawthorne is national . . ." Miller, *Dwelling Place*, 273.

p. 63, "a set of wearisome old souls . . ." Hawthorne, *Portable Hawthorne*, 306.

p. 63, "He possessed no power . . ." Ibid., 308.
p. 64, "could not help questioning . . ." Mellow, *His Times*, 314.
p. 65, "of the debt we owe you . . ." Turner, *A Biography*, 190.
p. 66, "I hereby take shame . . ." Hawthorne, *The Scarlet Letter*, 13.
p. 65, "Do let us try . . ." Ibid.

CHAPTER SEVEN: "Thoroughly Imbued with Ink"
p. 68, "A ray of sunshine . . ." Hawthorne, *Portable Hawthorne*, 635.
p. 69, "God will give him blood . . ." Mellow, *His Times*, 352.
p. 70, "he still is mentally engaged . . ." Ibid., 342.
p. 70, "so to speak, finished . . ." Ibid.
p. 71, "[T]he wrong-doing of one generation . . ." Ibid., 352.
p. 71, "[So] there he frisked about . . ." Nathaniel Hawthorne, *A Wonder Book for Boys and Girls* (Memphis: White Rose Press, 1987), 327.
p. 71, "I am going to begin . . ." Mellow, *His Times*, 364.
p. 72, "Down they went . . ." Hawthorne, *A Wonder Book,* 177.
p. 72 , "I now and then catch . . ." Hawthorne, *American Notebooks*, xxix.
p. 72, "more than mortal father . . ." Mellow, *His Times*, 376.
p. 72, "They have the pale tint . . ." Turner, *A Biography*, 231.
p. 73, "my last and latest . . ." Miller, *Dwelling Place*, 344.
p. 75, "should you spy . . ." Mellow, *His Times*, 392.
p. 76, "It would, indeed, be mortifying . . ." Ibid., 389.
p. 81, "It is only one-eyed people . . ." Turner, *A Biography*, 280.
p. 82, "I got upon my legs . . ." Ibid., 197.
p. 82, "an absurdly shy . . ." Ibid., 271.
p. 82, "The grim red-faced Monsters! . . ." Hawthorne, *Portable Hawthorne*, 9.
p. 83, "The toy-shops and the confectioners . . ." Mellow, *His Times*, 460.
p. 83, "Homeless on this foreign shore . . ." Hawthorne, *Portable Hawthorne*, 652.
p. 83, "our old home . . ." Turner, *A Biography*, 268.
p. 83, "When once a man . . ." Ibid., 273.

CHAPTER EIGHT: "The Devil Himself Always Seems to Get in My Inkstand"
p. 85, "America is now wholly given . . ." letter to Ticknor, Jan. 9, 1855
p. 85, "He can neither believe . . ." Turner, *A Biography*, 307.

p. 85, "I sleep ill . . ." Ibid., 317.

p. 85, "Thou *never* again shalt . . ." Mellow, *His Times*, 463.

p. 86, "If it were not . . ." Ibid., 464.

p. 86, "[L]ike every other abolitionist . . ." Ibid., 469.

p. 88, "Either the masques . . ." Ibid., 486.

p. 88, "If I had had a murder . . ." Ibid., 497.

p. 88, "vanishing bubbles" Ibid., 498.

p. 88, "The idea keeps returning . . ." Nathaniel Hawthorne, *The Marble Faun* (Boston: Houghton Mifflin Co., 1860), 70-73.

p. 89, "[I]f you come hither . . ." Ibid., 93.

p. 89, "Rest, rest, rest!. . ." Turner, *A Biography*, 375.

p. 91, "but the Devil himself. . . " Hawthorne, *Portable Hawthorne*, 15.

CHAPTER NINE: "I Have Not the Least Notion"

p. 94, "Heaven help me . . ." Ibid., 540.

p. 94, "[H]e is not an agreeable . . ." Turner, *A Biography*, 355.

p. 95, "What unimaginable nonsense . . ." Mellow, *His Times*, 547.

p. 97, "Though I think . . ." Ibid., 557.

p. 97, "I have now been a hermit . . ." Turner, *A Biography*, 377.

p. 98, "[S]o massive, not seemingly . . ." Hawthorne's journal, September 24, 1853.

p. 99, "Mr. Hawthorne's brain . . ." letter to Fields, February 25, 1864.

p. 100, "[H]e has wasted away . . ." Mellow, *His Times*, 574.

Bibliography

Bridge, Horatio. *Personal Recollections of Nathaniel Hawthorne*. New York: Haskell House Publishers, Ltd., 1968.

Brooks, Van Wyck. *The Flowering of New England*. New York: E.P. Dutton, 1936.

Bunyan, John. *Pilgrim's Progress*. Philadelphia: J.B. Lippincott Co., 1939.

Cantwell, Robert. *Nathaniel Hawthorne: The American Years*. New York: Rinehart & Co., Inc., 1948.

Hawthorne, Nathaniel. *The American Notebooks*. New Haven: Yale University Press, 1932.

———. *The Centenary Edition of the Works of Nathaniel Hawthorne*. 20 vols. Ed. Charvat, Pearce, Simpson, et al. Columbus: Ohio State University Press, 1962-1988.

———. *The Complete Novels and Selected Tales of Nathaniel Hawthorne*. New York: The Modern Library, 1937.

———. *The Complete Short Stories of Nathaniel Hawthorne*. New York: Hanover House, 1959.

———. *The House of the Seven Gables*. New York: Penguin Books, 1981.

———. *The Marble Faun*. Boston: Houghton Mifflin Co., 1860.

———. *The Portable Hawthorne*. Ed. Malcolm Cowley. New York: Viking Penguin, 1948.

———. *The Scarlet Letter*. New York: Penguin Books, 1983.

————. *Tales and Sketches*. New York: Literary Classics of the United States, Inc., 1982.

————. *A Wonder Book for Girls and Boys*. Memphis: White Rose Press, 1987.

Mellow, James R. *Nathaniel Hawthorne in His Times*. Boston: Houghton Mifflin Co., 1980.

Melville, Herman. *Redburn, White Jacket, Moby Dick*. New York: The Library of America, 1983.

Miller, Edwin H. *Salem Is My Dwelling Place: A Life of Nathaniel Hawthorne*. Iowa City: University of Iowa Press, 1991.

Tharp, Louise H. *The Peabody Sisters of Salem*. Boston: Little, Brown and Co., 1950.

Turner, Arlin. *Nathaniel Hawthorne: A Biography*. New York: Oxford University Press, 1980.

Weisman, Richard. *Witchcraft, Magic, and Religion in Seventeenth Century Massachusetts*. Amherst: The University of Massachusetts Press, 1984.

WEBSITES

Eldritch Press: Online Hawthorne Texts
http://www.eldritchpress.org/nh/hawthorne.html

Herman Melville and Nathaniel Hawthorne
http://www.melville.org/hawthrne.htm

The House of Seven Gables
http://www.7gables.org/

National Park Service: The Wayside Authors
http://www.nps.gov/mima/wayside/Hawth.htm

The Transcendentalists
http://www.transcendentalists.com/nathaniel_hawthorne.htm

Index